Zeppelins over the Eastern Counties

By
Cliff Clover

Part of the
Once Upon A Wartime Series No 17

Edited by Molly Burkett

Best Wishes Vic
With Thanks
Cliff Clover

First published by Barny Books,

ISBN No: 1.903172.65.9

Publishers: Barny Books
Hough on the Hill,
Grantham,
Lincolnshire
NG32 2BB

Tel: 01400 250246
Email: Barnybooks@hotmail.co.uk

A vote was passed at the Hague Conference in 1899 prohibiting aircraft from discharging projectiles or explosives.

The first Zeppelin was being built and was finally completed and launched on July, 2nd 1900. It was thought that if there was a war, Germany would use their Zeppelins to bomb Britain. In 1914 those fears were realised.

Count Ferdinand von Zeppelin in 1900

Count Ferdinand Von Zeppelin was born on the 8th of July, 1838. His family lived at the Castle of Girsliery on Lake Constance. The weather and water was an important part of his life and the young Von Zeppelin was interested in both from an early age and, as he grew older, this interest spread to engineering, mechanics and science. He had an enquiring mind and a tutor who taught him the powers of observation.

At the age of eighteen, he went to the Military College at Ludwigsburg but, although he qualified as an officer, he did not like the discipline and formality of the army, particularly the drill so he took a year out and went to Tubingen University to study engineering. Following that, he was posted to the Engineer Corps. He travelled widely and, in 1863, he was given permission to go to America. It was at the time of the Civil War and because of his rank and family wealth, he was treated as an important guest. He met Abraham Lincoln and was given permission to ascend in one of the army's observation balloons.

It changed his life. He realised straight away how valuable balloons could be on army manoeuvres but he also thought about the valuable contribution they could make to civilian life. He recognised that such developments depended on finding a suitable engine. He himself developed a light steam engine and a screw propeller but it wasn't until the French Military Balloon Establishment built a semi-rigid dirigible, La France, that he knew his ideas and dreams were possible.

He had long realised that the concept of non-rigid airships (i.e. without any framework to maintain the shape of the gas bag) was extremely limited and so turned his attention to the design of a rigid vessel.

This would have a structural skeleton over which the outer cover would be fitted and in which the gas for lifting the airship would be held in a series of gas bags (or ballonets) to the inside of the frame. This had the advantage that they could be filled and emptied individually and, also, leaks or puncture in one cell would not lead to catastrophic failure which could be the case with a non-rigid airship.

He also calculated that a rigid frame would allow for greater size and lifting power but he also realised that his plans were reliant on a suitable engine and, until Gottlieb Daimler perfected the gasoline engine, none had existed.

1908 Maybech 6 cyclinder side valve LZ4 engine 180hp @ 1200rpm
Started by pumping fuel air into cylinders while cranking
a hand start magneto

He had returned to the German Army in 1890 and tried to use his influence to gain help in developing his airship programme but the authorities didn't share his enthusiasm. Flying through the air in a balloon was a fairy tale to them and too often the answer was that if God had wanted us to fly he would have given us wings. But Count Zeppelin persevered. He became known as the Crazy Count because of his persistence. People would mock him in the streets of Stuttgart and children shouted after him.

The Count had one particular strength. He was able to select the right man for the right job. He enlisted aid and advice from the experts. He knew he needed to find a good engineer and he appointed Theodore Kober. Kober started on the design plans for the LZ1. It took three years to design. It was 420 feet long and 38 feet in diameter. Gas containers (known as ballonets) carrying 400,000 cubic feet of hydrogen were carried inside a rigid frame and the whole was driven by two 16 horsepower motors.

The Count needed a floating shed for the construction of the air ship so that it was easy to swing round. With the sealed end facing the wind, the airship could be brought out without being buffeted by the cross winds which incidentally, could have produced static electricity, a real fire hazard.

His application for a grant to build it was turned down time and time again. Eventually the Association of German Engineers came to his aid and a committee of experts were appointed to co-operate with Zeppelin. The shed was built with their help. The craft they were building became known as Luftschiffahrt (Airship) Zeppelin 1 - shortened to LZ1.

Zeppelin about to enter the floating shed

The LZ1 contained 24 aluminium girders, 16 gas containers of rubberised cloth to hold approximately 400,000 cubic feet of hydrogen. The outer envelope was made of cotton. Two petrol 16h.p. motors drove two vertical propellers for propulsion and two horizontal ones to assist, (in addition to a sliding weight) with ascent and descent.

The first flight was on the 2nd of July 1900. Crowds of people gathered along the lakeside to see what happened. Many were still sceptical about the idea of flying through the air. The flight lasted eighteen minutes before the airship was forced to land on the water. The fourth Zeppelin, LZ 4, however was a success. It made a twelve-hour flight to Switzerland and back. Zeppelin became an immediate celebrity.

Zeppelin LZ3 in flight in 1909

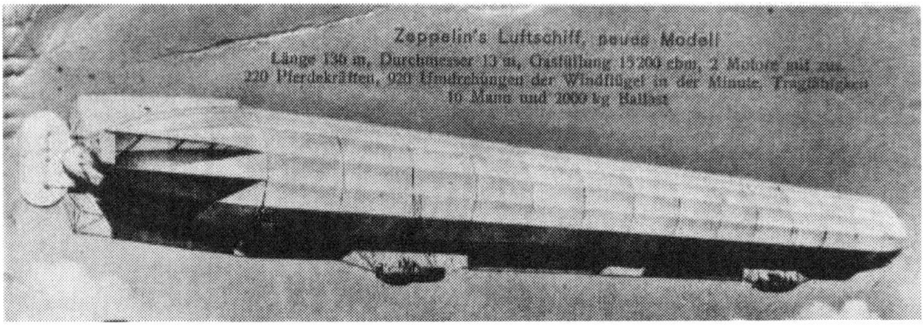

LZ4 on its maiden flight 20th June 1908

One of his greatest critics was Dr Hugo Eckener, a journalist with particular interest in aircraft and scientific matters. The Count went to his home to see him and appointed him as his flight director. Eckener became one of the greatest airship pilots in the world.

L to R at front: Hauptmann Kuno Manger, Dr Hugo Eckener, Count Zeppelin, Hermann Kraushaar and Rudolph Westphal

Early passenger Zeppelins in double hangar

War was declared on the 4th August, 1914. The first Zeppelin raid took place on the 6th August. The Army Z6 which had been used to carry passengers before war was declared, set out to bomb the fortress of Lutetia at Liege. There was low cloud and the airship was forced to fly low, so low in fact that it was hit by rifle fire. She was badly holed and failed to make her base near Bonn crashing in a forest near Cologne.

Although it caused little damage, it was a warning to the authorities of the danger that could come from the air and the British navy immediately requisitioned a Parseval airship, for training purposes.

PL25 were purchased to train our airship crews

LZ7 Passenger cabin – 1910

Before the war, passenger-carrying Zeppelins had run regular services. The commercial service was known as DELAG. Compartments that looked like railway carriages had been fitted to the frame and could carry twenty passengers. When the war broke out, these airships were transferred for military use, so were their crews, who were all naval personnel who had been selected for their powers of endurance.

Passenger Zeppelin showing railway carriage type accommodation

They were naval personnel from the High Seas Fleet who had proved their ability to withstand sickness, cold and wet conditions. They had also shown that they possessed common sense, comradeship and had the ability to think quickly and with responsibility. None of them were conscripted. They were all volunteers and there was no difficulty in finding them. Air travel was the wonder of the world at that time and there were many men that wanted the chance to fly. They all became officers or N.C.O.s.

The Zeppelins carried crews of 16 to 22 men according to the size of the ship (see appendix 1 for more details). The first Zeppelins used in the war carried two gondolas with a catwalk between them. The captain would be in the first one and the executive officer (his deputy) in the rear one. The captain had a speaking tube so that he could keep in touch with his deputy. The deputy was responsible for walking the airship in and out of the hangar, conveying orders from the commander to the men and arranging watch duties etc.

L1, the German Navy's first Zeppelin

Early gondola

Interior view of a Zeppelin gondola, showing the powerful Maybach motors in the centre receiving attention from engineers. On the left the look-out man and machine gun operators are seen ready to repel hostile aircraft. One of the large radiators for the water-cooled engines is situated just above their heads, while at their feet is a fire-extinguisher. At the rear of the gondola is a reserve steering apparatus.

Radio room - Note trailing aerials on drums under the bench. These could be let down by hand but wound in when flying through storms

View of the silence room in the centre cabin of a Zeppelin. This was insulated from the noise of the engine so they could call base and the radio centre without too much distraction

Wheeling out the gondola (early Zeppelin – L4 to L9)

The Chief Engineer was in charge of the mechanics, steersmen, machine gun operators and sail maker as well as supervising the smooth running of the airship. The Observation Officer was in charge of the wireless/telegraph operation, bombing equipment etc. The wireless operator sent and received messages. There were two steersmen, the elevator operator who managed the elevators which directed the airship's height and the rudder operator who directed the rudders which gave directional flight to the Zeppelin. They also managed the hydrogen valves and ballast release.

The sail-maker was responsible for all the gas cells and outer cover and the gas automatic release valves and manual valves. He would have to stitch and repair all torn fabric. There was a catwalk along the roof of the ship and he was lowered from this on a rope and repaired the fabric while the ship was in motion. He had to walk this every hour, night and day to check on any repairs that needed doing. It was often bitterly cold and he would walk along the catwalk with his hands in his pockets. One sail maker was lifted five feet into the air by a strong wind.

The catwalk of L6

There was also an observation car operator and relief crew on board. Hammocks were swung above the catwalk which was fitted inside the envelope and ran its whole length. Members of the crew could rest there when they were off duty.

When a raid was to take place, an order would be given to prepare the airship. They had about two hours from the time of the order until the take off. The airships were always kept ready for action and as much as possible had already been done. The huge double doors of the hangars would be opened and the handling crews would be standing by their craft. Hydrogen gas would hiss into the gas tanks (the ballonets), leaving a sickly sweet smell in the air. The envelope was hauled tight and mechanics would test run the engines, causing miniature whirlwinds to whirl high in the blast of air from the propellers.

The fuel, machines guns and ammunition and anything else that was needed for the raid was already in place.

Then the bombs had to be hung in position. They were brought out from the armoury in hand carts. The light calibre bombs were carried on board by the airship's care and maintenance party and placed in the corridor which ran the whole length of the ship inside the envelope. The medium and heavy calibre bombs had to be lifted into position with the help of tackle and were suspended from hooks to the bomb frames which were situated in the centre to ensure weight was distributed equally. Many of the bombs loaded would be incendiaries. Some of the crew would have prepared bombs of their own which would hang on little parachutes as they were dropped over England. On the later models from 1915, each Zeppelin would carry one huge bomb (300 kilograms).

Two burnt out incendiary bombs hanging in place, found in Lowestoft April 16, 1915

Flares were also carried for target searching together with smoke bombs which were set to detonate soon after leaving the Zeppelin to produce dense smoke to hide the Zeppelin from aircraft or searchlights or anti-aircraft fire.

Top half of a bomb dropped from a Zeppelin

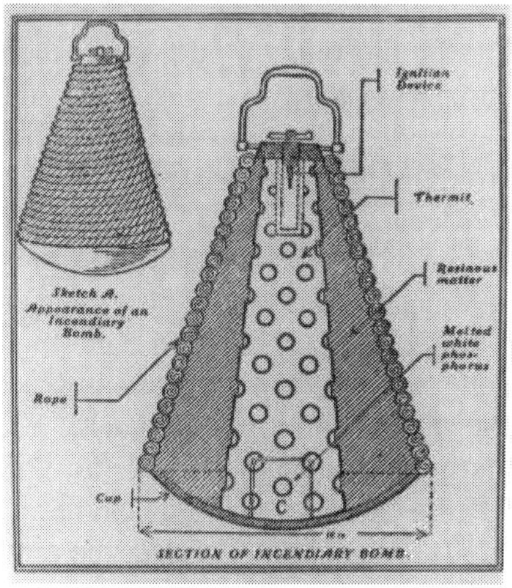

The Zeppelin Incendiary bomb. In addition to explosive bombs the Germans used incendiary bombs. One of the materials was Thermit, which generated intense heat (over 5000°F)

Bombs carried by Naval Zeppelins. In order of size these are 660lb, 220lb, 110lb and 22lb and a pair of incendiaries in the cart to the right and left. The men are holding bomb-fuses and a parachute flare stands in front of the 660-pounder

The air crews got ready for the raid by putting on their warm, fur-lined clothing and preparing their thermos flasks and taking their life-belts which was about all they were allowed to take. The space in the control and engine gondolas was so restricted that even their life belts had to be especially designed so that they fitted flat on the body. They would inflate in water. The crew would go for their final meal before take off and collect their packets of bread, butter and sausage and have their flasks filled. Their uniforms and the contents of their pockets were checked to make sure that they had nothing metal in their possession. Even metal buttons had been replaced and the gold or silver braid had been cut off the officers' uniforms. Fire and static electricity was a big fear. When an airship landed, the crew would stand well back from the envelope to avoid electrical shocks. There had been cases of men being electrocuted. On one occasion, the braid on the captain's cap started flashing with static electricity.

Every man would be weighed with every article that they would be carrying. Weight was important. Each airship had to be balanced so that it could float, motionless in the air. It had to be in a state that was known as neutral buoyancy. She was loaded with weights corresponding to the lift – the crew, the petrol, the guns and bombs etc and the water ballast. The total weight of the air ship itself plus those additional weights had to be adjusted exactly so that they equalled the amount of lift. This was fine tuned by altering the amount of ballast. Enough had to be carried to ensure that the ship did not have a tendency to rise or sit too heavily on the ground. When the ship was properly balanced, she floated in the air and two men were strong enough to push her up or pull her down. When this state of buoyancy had been achieved, then she was ready to be brought out of her hangar.

L22 brought into her hangar at Tondern after smashing her nose on the shed door, April 17, 1916

Inside LZ38 looking forward
Shows a Parabellum machine gun

The control car of the LZ38

2nd man from left of picture is the elevator man at the control wheel looking at the altimeter. Next is the rudder man in bow of car with bomb site on the right hand side. Commanding officer is using the speaking tube to contact the bomb room.
Machinist descending the ladder

The crews on the early airships had no protection at all. They raided in all weather. It was a five or six hour journey across the North Sea in temperatures as low as –30° Fahrenheit. The temperature decreased with height and could drop to -40ºF.

When the Commander arrived, the officer on duty would report that all was ready. A whistle would be blown summoning the handling party. They would take hold of the rails that ran along the bottom of the gondolas. With the order, "Airship forward," they would carry the huge ship, as large as an ocean liner, carefully out of the shed. The runners on the gondolas ran along steel rails and men on the trailing guide ropes controlled the airship.

Signals were given with flags. At the order of "hands off" and "ease up the guys", the landing party stepped back and the huge Zeppelin rose into the air. The Commander ordered, "Motors full speed ahead," and the Zeppelin, along with others that were on the raid, set sail for England.

In the control car of LZ 16. Left to right; commanding officer, Hans-Karl Gayer; head of training, Erich Blew; executive officer, Kurt Dehn.

Both the German army and navy had airship sections. Army airship numbers were preceded by LZ and the Naval airships by L. The army used theirs over the battle fields and the navy used theirs against shipping. Four months after war was declared, twenty five navy crews were in training or fully trained and nine bases were set up along the German coast with 3,740 officers and men stationed at them.

The airships were well armed for an attack. The control gondola and the rear gondola each had two parabellum machine guns. There was a tail gun position and on the top platform, three machine guns were positioned. The L42 also had a machine gun platform underneath the envelope.

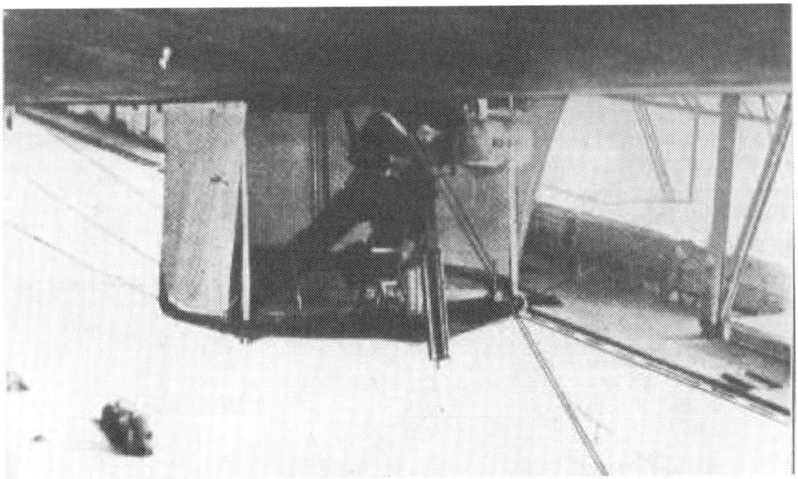

L42 machine gun platform built by the crew in order to repel attacks by aircraft

A Parabellum machine gun

Machine-gun mounted at rear tail position of later Zeppelins

The Zeppelins carried out raids in Europe but, at the beginning of the war, they were mostly used for reconnaissance purposes. On August the 17th the L3 carried out the first long distance flight, flying a 300-mile radius of Skagerrak searching for reported British warships.

There was a proposal to raid England but several Zeppelins had been damaged and destroyed and the idea was shelved. Meanwhile the allies were only too aware of their danger. On the 17th of September, the Home Secretary made an order, under the Defence of the Realm Act, to reduce all lighting in towns and over bridges, etc to render them less conspicuous from the air.

L15's forced landing outside the Nordholz base on the morning after the 13 October 1915 raid on London

Several raids were made by allied aeroplanes in an attempt to destroy the Zeppelins sheds. On the 8th October 1914, Lt. Marix, R.N.A.S. took off in a Sopwith Tabloid, no.168. It was a dull misty morning but it cleared later. He flew 112 miles from Antwerp and destroyed the Zeppelin, LZ9, in her shed. Marix was awarded the D.S.O. for this exploit.

Sopwith Tabloid

At 1.20 that day, Spenser-Grey took off in a Sopwith Tabloid, no. 167 but failed to locate the airship sheds so he bombed the railway yard and returned to base at 4.45 p.m.

The following day, Lt. Marix took off at 1.30 p.m. and flew at 1,000 feet and located the airship sheds. He dropped two bombs on them and caused an explosion, the flames shooting five hundred feet into the air. Marix was shot at but he escaped only to run out of fuel twenty miles from base. He managed to land and borrowed a bike and later a car to get back. The Germans captured the grounded plane and, later that same day, the base. The R.N.A.S. personnel escaped to Ostend.

On October the 19th, 1914 the first Zeppelin to approach England was sighted off Yarmouth flying North. It was next seen from Mablethorpe. In the following months several Zeppelins flew over the countryside but they didn't drop bombs. They were observing and reporting back. The Kaiser had forbidden the airships to drop any bombs on England. Kaiser Wilhelm was the grandson of Queen Victoria and wanted to protect his own family. His views were shared by other members of the German government who shared the Victorian view that women and children should always be protected.

Grand Admiral von Tirpitz, the Secretary of State for the Imperial Navy stated that the English were now in terror of our Zeppelins, perhaps not without reason.

"I am not in favour of frightfulness, also the indiscriminate dropping of bombs is wrong. They are repulsive when they hit women and children" he said.

Although German airships did not bomb England, the German aeroplanes did. A German seaplane appeared over Dover and dropped two bombs near the Admiralty pier. Both landed in the sea. Three days later, another German plane appeared over Dover Castle and dropped a bomb which landed in a cabbage patch. This was the first bomb to land on British soil.

On December 28th 1914, the Spalding Guardian reported that the first Zeppelin raid against a civilian target had been made on Nancy in France. Sixteen bombs had been dropped and two people had been killed.

On the 7th of January 1915, a fleet of Zeppelins with support aircraft was reported flying between Calais and Ghent. The Chief Constable of Norfolk immediately issued a naked light warning stating instant arrest and the possibility of being shot at by the civil guard or military patrols. Evacuation procedures in the event of invasion landings were also printed.

The chiefs of the German Naval War Staff, Admirals Rachman and von Pohl pressed the Kaiser to allow the Zeppelins to raid England. He finally approved limited attacks but only on military targets or docks. London was to be left alone. He insisted that bombing was to take place at nights and weekends when women and children would be safely at home.

On the 19th of January 1915, a young man saw what he thought were two bright stars. Then he realised that they were moving towards him and he saw their dark shapes in the sky. He lived at Ingham in Norfolk, about one and a half miles inland from the coast. Then he heard the roar of their engines and he knew that two of the frightening Zeppelins were flying above him. He was frightened and with cause. Zeppelins were the biggest objects that had ever been seen in the sky, 518 feet (158 metres) in length and 48½ feet (14.9metres) in diameter and they were noisy. Their three or four engines could often be heard roaring across the empty sky before they could be seen. As they came overhead, they separated. L3 turned south before reaching Stalham and flew towards Great Yarmouth. Lights were shining there and, as soon as the airship was over the target, the crew started to drop bombs.

L3 being walked into hangar, notice open gondolas

Meanwhile L4 made north west to Bacton and continued overland to Cromer. The wind swung it out over the sea. The Commander swung the ship to the left, this brought it over Sheringham which was displaying lights. It was flying very low and people ran out of their houses thinking that it was going to hit the rooves of their houses. It dropped one high explosive bomb which failed to explode and several incendiary bombs which caused some fires. One of these fell through the roof of the cottage, damaging the stairs before burying itself in the floor. The couple were eating their supper downstairs while the baby slept upstairs. None of them were disturbed. The airship then flew out to sea until the lights of Hunstanton were sighted. It flew over Thornham village. By this time it was flying so low that the control car almost hit the school bell tower and the villagers who had ventured out saw the faces of the crew looking out. One incendiary was dropped at Thornham and one at Brancaster. It then circled over Hunstanton where bombs were dropped on the wireless station which was tuned in to listen to the Zeppelin transmissions. It flew south and over Heacham where another incendiary bomb was dropped, this fell into a water butt standing outside the back door of a cottage.

At 10.50.p.m. she approached Kings Lynn. Seven high explosive bombs and seven incendiaries were dropped on Kings Lynn. Two people, Mrs Olive Smith and Mrs Gayley were killed and 13 injured. Houses were damaged. The dock engine house was hit, as was the railway power station.

The Zeppelin then made for home where she reported being attacked by A/A gunfire while being held in searchlights. This was incorrect. Neither Zeppelin was attacked and there were no searchlights in the area.

Press censorship kept news of the raid from the public to prevent mass panic.

Members of both crews were awarded Iron Crosses but neither Zeppelin survived to raid England again. They were brought down by storms in the North Sea and heavy layers of snow which weighed them down. L3 came down and the 16 crew were interned for the rest of the war, L4 came down near the shore and eleven of the crew jumped into the sea and waded ashore which made the airship lighter and she was able to lift into the air again and was blown out to sea with four members of the crew still on board. They were never heard of again.

Wrecked houses in Kings Lynn,
note hole in foreground made by the bomb

Zeppelins L3 and L4 carried out the first airship raids on England bombing Great Yarmouth and Kings Lynn, Norfolk. A third Zeppelin was forced to turn back. It was a damp day with squalls of rain and snow as the Zeppelins approached at eight o'clock in the evening flying at 300 feet. Twenty-five bombs were dropped (2,155 pounds). Two people were killed in Yarmouth and four in Snettisham. Sixteen people were injured. The local paper reported that there was a hole near Snettisham Church big enough to take a horse and cart. The Church windows were broken.

The crater near Snettisham church

People were out in the street in Great Yarmouth, attracted outside by the engine noise and excited at seeing the outlines of these great machines in the sky. Two bombs were dropped alongside St. Peter's Church killing an elderly lady, Mrs Martha Taylor, who had gone out to fetch her supper. Mr Smith, a middle-aged shoemaker who had gone out to watch the Zeppelin was also killed. Houses were wrecked and a steam drifter in the river was damaged. The borough engineer managed to extinguish the lights as the airship set off for its return journey. This was the first Zeppelin raid on English soil.

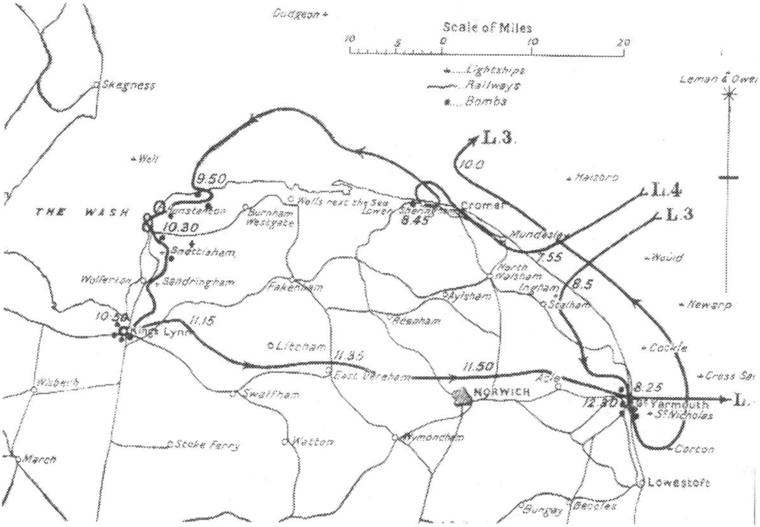

The map shows the paths of the two Zepplins which carried out the first German raid on Great Britain 19/20th January 1915. Black dots denote where the bombs landed.

L3 which with L4, was the very first Zeppelin to raid England on January 19/20 1915.

L3 bombed Gt Yarmouth, L4 dropped bombs on Sheringham, Hunstanton, Snettisham and Kings Lynn

The house in St Peter's Plain, Gt. Yarmouth that was damaged in the first Zeppelin raid.

The house today. There is a plaque above the door

Close up of the placque on previous page which reads: "The First House in Great Britain to be damaged by a Zeppelin Air Raid 19th January 1915"

5th February - the Spalding Guardian reported a powerful single seater-racing car driving around Weston Hill area with a powerful central mounted headlamp at night. (It was never traced).

Rumours like this mounted. People were suspicious of any stranger in their area thinking they were spies. The police received many reports of strange lights at night or out at sea and unusual noises at nights. Few people had seen an aeroplane let alone an airship and householders did not have telephones in those days or electric lights. With so many men away at war, women were on their own. The Zeppelins frightened them and the thought of being bombed terrified them. Imaginations ran riot. A report of men marching through a village during the night proved to be a herd of cows that had broken down a fence and escaped from the field. Reports of strange lights in the woods near Grantham were sites where marsh gas escaped. A rumour spread in Grimsby that two spies had been caught in the Admiralty wireless telegraphic station in Humberstone Avenue. The two spies turned out to be two of the workmen who were working on the unfinished building.

Captain Ernst Lehmann was guiding his Zeppelin, Army LZ12, through thick cloud on March 16th, 1915 but couldn't locate his target because of the poor visibility. He decided to design an observation car which could be lowered below the clouds and the occupant could see the terrain beneath them and guide the captain.

The first observation car he made was a simple affair made from a butter tub or barrel with a small anti-spin fin. A crew member sat in this contraption and was lowered 900 feet below the Zeppelin by a hand operated winch.

Peter Strasser, Head of the Naval Airship Division, heard of the device and decided that he wanted to try it out for himself. On the 23rd of March, 1915, he climbed into the tub and was lowered by the hand winch. A strong wind was blowing and it caught the tub and swung it rearwards.It became tangled with one of the landing ropes. The winch-man wasn't aware of what was happening and he continued winding out the rope until it extended for the full 900 feet. The tub untangled itself in the strong wind and fell like a stone to the full 900 feet length of the rope and it began to spin rapidly, first in one direction and then in the other. It was some time before the winch-man could wind the tub back. A jaded Peter Strasser climbed out and decided then and there that there was no future in the idea of an observation car especially as it would take up precious weight that was needed for the bomb load.

Peter Strasser

A mark 2 vehicle was constructed with a much larger fin but it was still not popular with the crew. Mark 3 was a wickerwork canoe, covered in to protect the occupant from the bitter cold. 1,200 feet of quarter inch diameter of power cable was hollowed to allow telephone lines to be carried in it.

Mark 4 was fish shaped, made of alloy with a celluloid windscreen, a phone and 2,000 feet of cable. This was tested by von Gremmingham, one of Count Zeppelin's relations. A few improvements were made for Mark 5.

Mark 6 was introduced in mid 1916. The car was completely enclosed. The observer lay down in it and looked through a celluloid window. He had a chart table, a compass and an electric light. The cable contained phone and lighting cables and could extend for 3,000 feet. The total weight of the cable, winch, car and crew member was 540 pounds and the length, including the fins, was 14 feet.

They soon became known as Cloud Cars and were not the most popular job for the crew member although it had one saving grace, the operator could have a cigarette, something that was never allowed on board an airship. It had many downsides.

When getting into the car, the observer had to step over space and climb into it while it was moving. At the same time, he could see the axe ready to chop through the cable if the Zeppelin was attacked or hit trouble and the Zeppelin needed to climb in a hurry. Losing 540 pounds of weight would be a great help in those circumstances. It was extremely cold in the car and the swinging ride could make the observer sick.

A Mark 6 cloud car that is now part of the Imperial War Museum collection

On the 4th of March, L8 took off from Gontrobe with 70 bombs on board to attempt a raid on England. She was fired on by machine guns and crash landed at Tirlemont in Belgium as she attempted to return to Düsseldorf. One member of the crew was killed and several others were injured.

On March 26th, a council meeting was held in Spalding to discuss turning off the gas supply to quickly extinguish all lights in the event of a raid. (Little thought was given to what could happen when it was turned on again.)

In the following weeks, raids were reported at Maldon, Lowestoft, Faversham, Ipswich, Aldeburgh (looking for Stowmarket munitions works), Southend, the Humber, Ramsgate, Burnham on Crouch and Shoeburyness (although on one raid on the Humber, the airship, L5, suffered severe icing on the envelope and engine failure on two engines. She began to lose height and just managed to limp back to base after jettisoning her bombs and ballast).

Lowestoft Raid

Bomb crater, Lowestoft raid by L5 April 16th 1915

Navigation relied on sightings on the land. The Humber with its distinctive Spurn Bight and the Grimsby Dock Tower and the docks at Hull and Immingham made a clear point for the Zeppelin captains. They would cross the North Sea in daylight and stay out at sea near lightships waiting for nightfall.

The first raid over London was by LZ 38 piloted by Erich Linnarz. On May 31st, 1915, when, flying at 10,000 feet, it reached Finchley. Bombs killed two cows and some Indian soldiers when a billet was hit. An eight year old girl was killed walking home from the cinema and seven people were killed and twenty six injured when a bomb was dropped on Hoxton Street in the East End of London. Ninety incendiaries and thirty grenades were dropped. Nine aircraft took off to attack it without success. One of the aircraft crashed and the pilot was killed.

LZ38
Some impression of the size of this Zeppelin can be gauged from the crew members manning the machine gun post at the very top of the airship

The Kaiser reiterated that no historic buildings in London were to be bombed.

On the 4th of June, L10, piloted by Hirsch, came in over the Isle of Sheppey at 9p.m. bombing Gravesend and Sittingbourne in mistake for Harwich. The yacht club, military hospital, houses and stables were damaged. Twenty bombs were recorded (1,547 pounds) and £8,740 worth of damage. There were no deaths.

On the 6th of June a Zeppelin flew over Theddlethorpe and out to sea to Flamborough Head. Turning east, it bombed Hull, killing twenty four and injuring forty.

Hull, many buildings were destroyed and Holy Trinity Church, above, had a narrow escape.

L37 had to abort its raid on London because of strong headwinds and bad weather. It turned back and was brought down on its return flight, over Ghent, by Lt Warnford, flying a Morane at 6,000 feet who dropped six bombs on it. Twenty eight of the crew were killed but one survived. The airship had been shot down over St. Elizabeth's convent. The crewman survived by falling through the roof and landing on a bed. It wasn't occupied at the time.

No 1 Naval Aeroplane Squadron,
7th June, 1915

Wing Commander Longmore.

Sir,

I have the honour to report as follows:

I left Furtnes at 1.00a.m. on June 7th on Morane No. 3253 under orders to proceed to look for Zeppelins and attack the Bercham St. Agathe Airship Shed with six 20lb bombs.

On arriving at Dixmude at 1.05a.m. I observed a Zeppelin apparently over Ostend and proceeded in charge of the same. I arrived at close quarters a few miles past Bruges at 1.50 a.m. and the airship opened heavy Maxim fire so I retreated to gain height and the Airship turned and followed me.

At 2.15.a.m. he seemed to stop firing and at 2.25.a.m. I came behind, but well above the Zeppelin: height then 11,000 feet and switched off my engine to descend on top of him.

When close above him, at 7,000 feet, I dropped my bombs and, whilst releasing the last, there was an explosion which lifted my machine and turned it over. The aeroplane was out of control for a short period but went into a nose dive and the control was regained.

I then saw that the Zeppelin was on the ground in flames and also that there was something burning in the air all the way down. The joint on my pipe and petrol pump from the back tank was broken and at about 2.40a.m. I was forced to land and repair my pump.

I landed at the back of a forest close to a farmhouse; the district is unknown on account of the fog and the changing of course. I made preparations to set the machine on fire but apparently I was not observed, so was enabled to effect a repair and continued at 3.15a.m. in a south westerly direction after considerable difficulty in starting my engine single handed.

I tried several times to find my whereabouts by descending through the clouds but was unable to do so. So eventually I landed and found that it was at Cape Gris Nez and took in some petrol. When the weather was cleared I was able to proceed and arrived at the aerodrome about 10.30a.m.

As far as I could see, the colour of the airship was green on top and yellow below and there was no machine or gun platform on top.

I have the honour to be, Sir,
Your obedient servant,
R.A.J. Warneford,
Flt. Sub-Lieutenant.

R.A.J. Warneford's report. The Zeppelin he shot down was LZ37

On the 15th of June, L9 carried out a raid on the North east coast targeting, Northumberland, Tyneside, Wallsend, South Shields and Jarrow.

In July, the Harwich force (a navy patrol) spotted six Zeppelins on patrol in German Bight and Sopwith Schneider seaplanes attempted to take off to attack them but they all broke floats in the choppy seas and had to be hauled aboard by ships of the Harwich Naval North Sea Force which carried sea planes.

In mid-October 1915 there was a five Zeppelin raid on Norfolk, Suffolk, the Home Counties and London.

It was often difficult for the Zeppelin captain to know exactly where he was or if there were any dangers ahead, particularly on a dark night. On 14th 0f October, 1915, L 13 and L 14 were returning to base when they almost collided with each other over Oxted and then again above Woolwich ferry. The passengers on the ferry were terrified. They could make out dark shapes above them and wondered what was happening. It was thought that the envelopes of the two airships actually touched before they drew apart.

A Naval Zeppelin, SL2, was returning from a raid in the London area when it experienced engine trouble and was forced to return to base on one engine. She was wallowing over the sea, flying lower and lower. The crew were relieved to see the coast of Belgium but still the airship went down and down until it settled on the roof of a cottage and the chimney protruded into the Zeppelin. It became apparent almost immediately that the occupants had a good fire going. Some of the crew clambered down the ropes, rushed into the cottage and put out the fire with what came to hand. They saved the airship. They lifted it off the chimney the next morning and managed to get back to base.

The problem that faced the British aircraft was that they could not climb as quickly or fly at such a great altitude as the Zeppelins. Zeppelins could gain height at a thousand feet a minute. Our fighter planes needed ten minutes to gain the same height. Unless the airships were forced to fly low, generally because of poor weather conditions, the pilots could not get above them and drop their bombs on the envelope.

Lack of oxygen and the extreme cold experienced at high altitudes were problems for the crews. Thermometers froze, compasses stopped working and engines stuttered and died. British aircraft could not function above 13,000 feet. Some German airships were lost because the crews were unable to cope with the conditions. Men stuffed newspapers in their flying suits but many still suffered from frostbite. Even when they solved these problems, there was another one that beat them, the weather. The wind could be so strong that the airships could be difficult to handle and they would be blown off course. Snow and ice forming on the envelope would add so much weight that the Zeppelins were forced down lower, bringing them within range of the British guns. The crews could not escape the oil and exhaust fumes or the sickening smell of the hydrogen. On one raid, two members of the crew in the gondola died from carbon monoxide poisoning.

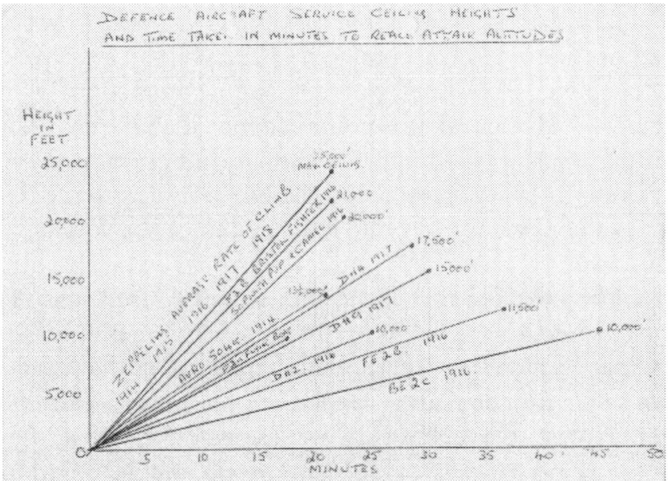

Graph comparing Zeppelin against aeroplanes in time taken to reach height, Zeppelin line on extreme left taking 20 minutes to reach 25,000 feet

The first raid of 1916 took place on the night of 31st January. It was a dark, foggy night with rain and snow showers as the nine Zeppelins approached the Humber. L13 made for Hull docks and bombed warehouses and the dock crane. It then went on to demolish Redbourne Ironworks before making for Scunthorpe. L20 dropped bombs in the Grantham area before making for Loughborough. L15 bombed Boston.

Captain Dietrich was in command of L21. It came in over Norfolk making for the midlands and started to drop bombs on Walsall. There was not a full black out in the town and men climbed lamp-posts trying to extinguish the gas lights. One bomb landed on some public toilets as a tram was passing and the glass in the windows shattered. Mary Slater, the Mayoress of Walsall, was travelling on the tram with her sister and sister in law and she was hit in the throat by a piece of glass. She was taken to hospital but died from her injury on February the 20th.

It was soon after this that press censorship was imposed to prevent mass panic.

We were coming out of St. Andrews Church after evening service when we saw this Zeppelin flying fairly low over Walsall. We could hear it more clearly than we could see it because it was a dark night. People climbed the lampposts to try and extinguish the gas lights. The Zepp was obviously attracted by the lights and dropped a bomb. A tram was passing at that moment and the blast broke its windows. A piece of the glass struck the Mayoress who was riding in the tram and she died from her injuries. The Zeppelin then went on and bombed Lichfield.

Mrs Braugh

Although there was a lot of Zeppelin activity around the Boston area, no bombs were ever dropped on the docks. This was because it was agreed that this could be the port through which British and German prisoners of war, who were no longer fit for military service, could be exchanged. They were carried by Dutch ships, Holland being a neutral country in the First World War. 2,582 people (2,136 soldiers and 446 civilians) were brought home from Germany and a similar number of Germans were repatriated. Sixteen Boston trawler men were in the first party that arrived in January, 1918, along with two hundred and thirty five crippled soldiers.

Bostonians didn't only have to fear attacks from the air. The Boston trawler, Porpoise, which was based at Grimsby was sunk in the Wash by a German U-boat after the crew had been ordered off and taken prisoner. They spent the rest of the war as Prisoners of War in Germany and it was a long time before their families knew what had happened to them. The Skipper was Billy Heaton and the 2nd chief officer was Mr Warsop. There were six men in the crew.

All of January had been good weather. It was on the Monday when the Zepps came in over the Wash at a quarter to five, just as it was getting dark. Everywhere was blacked out. My old Dad and uncle had gone to Sleaford market that day and I was left in charge. That meant I had to shut up the chickens. Living near the railway lines like we did, we knew that no trains were running so we didn't expect them back till morning.

The sky seemed full of engines. There were Zeppelins all about us. The pheasants didn't like being disturbed. They had gone to roost and they set up one hell of a racket. I never knew we had so many pheasants about.

My old pal came up the road on his bike and he was half scared out of his wits. He was breathing heavy like and muttering that he had seen them. Like big silver cigars he said they were. I said I'd wished I'd seen them but he said I wouldn't say that if I knew what they were like. They'd given him such a shock that he'd fallen off his bike.

Dad turned up O.K. the next morning. He said all the trains had been stopped when the air raid warning sounded.

Mr Sills, Boston.

January 31st 1916. Sixteen Zeppelins had set out that night to raid England. Four hundred and thirty six bombs were dropped including sixty on London. Four people were killed and twelve injured.

The forward gondola of a later model of the German naval airship showing the open control car. The control car looks like one gondola but is actually two separate ones with panels joining them. This reduced the engine noise and vibration transmitted to the forward car and wireless cabin.

It was the first time that Boston civilians had been seriously affected by bombing and rumours started to spread as to why they had been raided. There was a German family called Cantenwein who had been running a baker's business for two generations and were well liked in the town. There was an ale house on the opposite bank and one of the men who had been drinking there on the night of the raid reckoned that he had seen a light at the bakery and that the German family had been signalling to the Zeppelin. The rumours spread until a crowd collected and marched on the shop, breaking the windows and destroying property. The family managed to escape and hide and, later on, they were returned to Germany in one of the repatriation ships that left Boston. The light that the drinker saw was the reflection from a candle.

My Dad worked in the steelworks at Scunthorpe and he came home one night at the end of January, (January 31st 1916) and said that there'd been a warning put out that a Zeppelin was flying round North Lincolnshire. Well my mother went into a right undertaking, sure that we were all going to be killed in our beds and thinking we ought to take what we could and hide out in the fields until the morning. My father laughed and said that they were after the chemical works, not houses like ours and they'd only drop bombs where the lights showed and you couldn't see any light through our curtains. Mother wasn't going to risk it. She turned the oil lamp down so low, we could hardly see what we were eating. Everywhere outside was dark too, even the street lamps had been turned off.

We sat there in the dark and we could hear explosions out in the country and it sounded as if they were coming nearer and my Mother wasn't the only one that was frightened. We all were. Then the noise stopped and we guessed the airship had gone. Mother sent us all to bed but, about two hours later, we were woken up by this noise and it sounded as if a train was going to come through the bedroom. Then there was this echoing boom and Agnes said it was a bomb. The war had come to Scunthorpe.

The first bomb dropped on Ravendale Street and destroyed four houses. We could see lights and hear explosions as bombs and incendiaries were dropped all round us. One fell on Widow Markham's house. We all knew her. Her husband Enoch Markham had started the Scunthorpe Co-operative

Society. Old Widow Markham threw a bucket of water over the bomb and a neighbour threw it out of the window.

Two bombs were dropped near the North Lincoln works and another hit the Redbourn Hill works. Two workmen were killed, Thomas Danson of Scunthorpe and Jack Cyril Wright of Ashby. Another bomb fell near Dawes Lane killing Mr Wilkinson Benson of Scunthorpe. The airship was over the town for about ten minutes, dropping about 20 high explosive bombs and 50 incendiary ones as well as aerial torpedoes and although some were dropped near the chemical and the steel works, little damage was done.

You should have seen the people who had run into the countryside for shelter coming back the next morning. My Dad reckoned they'd taken everything with them bar the kitchen sink. They'd left their homes in such a hurry, they'd gather all sorts of things to take with them and forgotten some. One family found shelter in a barn out in the country before they realized that they'd forgotten the baby. The husband was despatched post-haste to fetch it but he must have forgotten a second time, because when he came back, he was wheeling the pig in a wheelbarrow and he'd had to go back again.

Thomas Lee

There was a nine Zeppelin raid on the 1st of February L19 ran out of fuel at about 3 a.m. on the return journey from a raid over England. It had approached Liverpool and overstayed which had made it short of fuel. It crashed into the sea and drifted west. At seven o'clock, it was sighted by a fishing boat - the King Stephen.

We left Newsand about two o'clock in the afternoon. The weather was fine. We steamed N.E. towards Hornsea about 90 miles out. We shot our gear at 3a.m. I was on watch at five o'clock and I saw a white, fixed light and then a flash light but it was a good way off. I called the skipper, (William Martin), and he said that we would haul in. After we got our gear in, we steamed towards the light and, as we got up to it, I could see what it was. It was a Zeppelin and men were sheltering on it. The top part was in the air and the other part was laid flat.

We went to windward of it and their skipper called out asking us to send a boat to rescue the men. There were about twenty five of them. The German skipper said that he would give us five pounds if we took them off but our skipper did not know what to do. He said that if he took them on board, they would take charge of his ship and we would become prisoners. He shouted back and said that he would go and get some help.

L19 Flight Path

The German crew were already half dead with shock, exhaustion and exposure. This was the first time they had flown the L19. They had previously been the crew of L9 also under the command of Captain Loewe. They had spent the last few hours writing messages to their families. The appearance of the King Stephen had been an answer to their prayers only for their hopes to be dashed when the boat turned away.

L9 landing at base in Belgium

It was about half past eight then so we set the course W by N. As we came in, we saw the Egret. She was towing. It was about one o'clock then. Our Skipper told them about the crashed airship. He thought the Egret would get her gear and steam out and take half the crew off each but the skipper of Egret couldn't see his way to do it, so we kept coming in.

The wind freshened during the night and we got under the land about half past nine and let her lay until the break of day when we came into Newsand.

The alert was then raised but it was too late. The airship had sunk and the whole German crew had perished. William Martin was blamed for their deaths and many fisher folk avoided him. He was distressed by what had happened and became ill. He died shortly afterwards.

With fifteen men on the upper platform, roof and body of L19 (minus cars) drifting at about longitude three degrees east. I am trying to write a final report. What with three engines broken down and a light head wind on the homeward flight, my flight was delayed and I got held up in fog over Lincolnshire where we were met by rifle fire. Ship became very heavy and three of our engines broke down simultaneously. Probably our last hour.

Feb 2nd 1916 at about 1.00 p.m. Lowe.
Bottle message picked up by Swedish yacht, Stell Smogen, three weeks later.

The second bottle to be picked up contained a message written by Observation Officer, Lieutenant Erwin Braunhof.

We have been drifting about two days and two nights. No help. Best wishes. An English steam trawler has refused to rescue us. Erwin.

The third message that was picked up was from a non commissioned officer.

My Dear Ada and Mother,

It is now about eleven o'clock on the morning of the 2nd of February. We are all still alive but we have nothing to eat. This morning an English steamer came up to us but refused to rescue us. It was the King Stephen from Grimsby.

My courage is ebbing away and the wind is growing fiercer. Your loving Hans who will think of you in heaven.

At 12.30. we all prayed together and bade each other goodbye. *Yours Hans.*

The King Stephen refusing to rescue the L19

Three Zeppelins set out to attack northern England on March the 5th, 1916. L11, L13 and L14 travelled overland from the Humber in a heavy snowstorm. The target was the Firth of Forth. A depression was approaching from Iceland which they hadn't expected and strong winds carried them much further south than they realised. Snow squalls battered them and they were covered with freezing slush. St. Elmo's fire (static electricity) flashed from the metal struts and joints and ice built up on the cover. When the clouds cleared a little, the Commander of L11, Captain Schutze, was surprised to see the city of Hull beneath him. He thought he was much further north but the distinctive pattern of the dark waters of the Humber and the snow covered docks and streets left him in no doubt of his position. Another Zeppelin was already over the city so Schutze held back until it had cleared the area. Then he went in and dropped his bombs. He dropped 3,600 pounds of bombs on the slumbering town. The first bomb dropped harmlessly in the Humber close to Earle's shipyard. Twenty more bombs destroyed houses and water mains and incendiaries set fire to the Mariners' almshouses and a shed in the docks.

Schutze reported seeing great fires and houses collapsing and people running from the flames.

As the L11 turned for home, her forward engine stopped. In the freezing temperature, the oil had congealed and the water in the radiator had frozen. One squall carried the airship 2,500 feet in two minutes before the crew managed to bring her under control, only for the elevator to jam and she rose to 10,500 feet before it was repaired. Then the after engine failed and the Zeppelin limped home on two engines.

The Zeppelin that Schutze had sighted over Hull had been the L14 under the command of Captain Bocker. He thought, too, that he was much further north when he sighted the dark streak of the Humber. Hull lay ahead. He dropped his first bombs near Beverly but they landed harmlessly in fields. He then dropped 7 explosive bombs and 13 incendiaries on Hull, damaging houses in the area of the docks. The wind was blowing further south. It was too strong to allow him to turn and make a second run over the city especially as two of his engines had stopped. Water in the petrol had frozen and he, also, had to limp back to base.

There was no opposition at all. No guns fired at the two Zeppelins and no planes went up to intercept the airships. The people of Hull did not disguise their feelings. They stoned a R.F.C. vehicle in Hull and a Flying Officer was mobbed in Beverly.

Bőcker, L14
Commander

A train travelling from Lincoln was bombed near Caythorpe. The following day was market day in Grantham and a farmer, Fred Parker, picked up three of the incendiary bombs, two of which were still live and took them to market with him in his trap. Going to lunch at the local inn, he left the pony harnessed with the trap in the yard.

On the night of March 31 / April 1 1916, seven Zeppelins set out to bomb England, one of which was L22 commanded by Captain Max Dietrich. It was a new airship and the engines had not been fully run in so it was slower than the other machines. The fleet of airships turned over the Lincolnshire coast making for London but L22, being that much slower, flew as far as Newark then turned for home. As it flew towards the coast at

Cleethorpes, there was a short burst of gun fire. The L22 turned over the town and dropped its bombs.

At first, the local people were not worried when they heard the Zeppelin overhead. Several airships had already flown along the Humber and inland over the town without trouble. This time was different. A stick of 25lb bombs were released, one of which scored a direct hit on the Baptist Chapel. Others fell in line along the sea front near Sea View Street, one of which hit the Council House.

Soldiers from the Manchester Regiment were billeted in the Chapel. They had only arrived in the town that day, bringing the number of troops in the area to two thousand, most of them billeted near the gasworks. They had been welcomed by a band and flags flying. They had marched to the Baptist Chapel where they were offered tea and cakes by the local people. Three of the men had only been recruited a few days earlier and two men were due for discharge as they had completed twenty-one years in the army. That the raid should have happened on the day the Manchesters had arrived was a stroke of misfortune. Thirty one soldiers were killed and only four of the others had escaped injury. (They had been playing cards in the cellar). The injured were treated in field hospitals that had been set up in local buildings. St Aidans Church was one of these.

St Aidan's Institute was taken over as a Voluntary Aid Detachment Hospital under the command of Mrs Ellis, an energetic and enthusiastic Church worker. Several doctors offered their services. It opened one Friday with 33 Belgian soldiers and, of course, being Belgian, they were all Catholic and they wanted fish. There were also four British soldiers and they didn't mind what they had. Small operations were carried out there like amputating fingers or toes and removing bullets or shrapnel. We tried to make them comfortable and feel at home especially at Christmas and we had four Christmases there. And all the time the Zeppelins were coming over. They were terrible and the men were terrified. The flashes would light up the Church roof. There was one really bad night and we discovered later that it had been at Scartho. Our Church would have been a wonderful target for the bombs but God was good and protected us.

It was the night of March 31st when we got an urgent call for help. A direct hit had been made on the Baptist Church. The call came from the Manchester Regiment depot. Mrs Carlton, Mrs Ellis, Miss Glover, Miss King, Mr Thrushell and myself set off with what we could carry leaving the Revd. Porter and Mr Overton in charge. We looked for a taxi but it took too long so we proceeded as best we could. The Zeppelin was overhead which wasn't very cheerful. We made our way to Yarra House. It was Dante's Inferno. Three rooms were covered with bodies, dead, dying and suffering. We did what we could. The first man I went to was dead. I offered to take men back and I asked for a telephone so that I could phone and ask them to get beds ready. We filled an ambulance and I went with it, mounting the box. We got as far as Isaacs Hill, we had such a load. I decided I would get there quicker if I walked. I hadn't gone far when I saw Cripsey's taxi. I held it up and sat in front with my hat in my hand and my boots unlaced and arrived at the hospital before the ambulance. They had been working. The beds were ready. We had thirteen men within half an hour. Drs Swindells, Grierson and Martin arrived to attend them. We admitted thirty six men that night. We didn't have time to stop for a cup of tea until half past seven. Got home to bed at 11.30. but called out again at 12.30. Caulfield had very bad gangrene set in.

The funeral was the following Tuesday – what a funeral, what a walk. There were three bands and three Regiments and a section of the navy. The first part of the procession was at the cemetery whilst the other was just leaving Poplar Road mortuary. The relatives were standing near the graves with the firing party in the centre. It was pretty safe until they started playing the Dead March during committal. They fainted, one after the other. We doubled up and ran across the field to help the poor souls, some husbands, some sons and some brothers, one widow only married six weeks. Then the firing party, very grand but terrible.

It is the first military funeral I've ever attended. I trust it will be the last.

Extract from hospital diary

Nurses at Cleethorpes
Back Row: Mrs Skelton, Mrs Earnshaw, Mrs Tilley, Miss Glover, Mrs Overton
Front Row: Dr Felton, Mrs Ellis, Miss Brown

British, French and Belgian soldiers in the Zeppelin Raid over Cleethorpes April 1st 1916

Cleethorpes Baptist Church
Destroyed by Zeppelin bomb, April 1st 1916

Extracts from log of L16:

I. April 1916.
Came in at Winterton and made for Bury St. Edmunds at midnight. Dropped bombs. Made for Lowestoft and home.

II. November 27 1916.
Bombed Wakefield, Chesterton and Barnsley. Spent 9 hours over England. Attacked by aircraft twice but escaped in cloud and darkness.

III. Winter 16/17.
Severe winter caused famine amongst troops marooned at garrison on North Sea island. L 16 diverted to carry supplies to them as ships could not reach them.

1916 was the year when bombing in England reached its peak. Vice Admiral Reinhard Scheer, the new Commander of the German High Seas Fleet was keen to increase the air ship attacks on Britain. The navy continued with their reconnaissance over the North Sea but they also flew frequent bombing missions, often being joined by army Zeppelins. By the end of the year, the airship Commanders found the British defences had improved. There were more searchlights and better artillery and the blackout was fully observed. As a result, the Germans failed to cause so much damage.

On the 25th of April 1916, a German U boat captured the King Stephen. The nine crew were taken prisoner and interrogated. They admitted their deep regret about what had happened to the crew of the L19. They were treated fairly and spent the rest of the war as Prisoners of War.

Lincoln provided a good navigation point for the Zeppelin commanders with its distinctive cathedral and, although it was bombed, very little serious damage was caused but one raid was the reason for a different kind of tragedy. There had been a raid on Saturday night, the 16th of September. A bomb was dropped on a garden in Washingborough and two or three in a field between the railway and the Lincoln to Greetwell Road.

A train sheltered in a cutting and came into the city when the Zeppelin cleared the area. The driver realised the Zeppelin was overhead and stopped the train beneath the bridge so the airship could not see the engine fire. He stayed there for what seemed a long time, worried because he knew he should not stop between stations and also that another train would run into him. The Lincoln station master claimed that when the train pulled in, the driver's hair had turned completely white.

Washingborough cut where the train stopped during the Zeppelin raid

Although nobody in Lincolnshire was injured, thirty six people were killed and one hundred and twenty six injured that night and two Zeppelins were brought down. The next day people from the city crossed to Washingborough on the ferry to view the damage but, on one of the return trips, the ferry that was overloaded turned over and two people were drowned, Ernest Robinson aged seventeen of Carlton Road, Lincoln and George Melson aged seven of Winnowsty Lane.

On May 2nd, 1916, the army Zeppelin LZ98 set out with seven other airships to raid the east coast. She came over the River Humber in heavy cloud at about 2,000 feet. The captain ordered that the observation car was lowered. A lady living at the top of the hill at Elsham Wold heard the Zeppelin approaching and ran out to bring the cat in when she heard a swishing noise. She forgot the cat and made for the back door and, at that moment, the observation car flew between the back door and the outside toilet. Obviously the crew in the Zeppelin hadn't realised there was a hill in the vicinity but they soon found out when the cloud thinned and the observation car was winched in.

Later that year, a man was cycling along the road near Gosberton when a cloud car was lowered and, for a short while, was travelling along beside him. The Zeppelin was lost and the observer asked directions for Grimsby. The cyclist was still shaking with shock when he reported the incident to the warden.

On July, 28th, a Friday night, two Zeppelins, L17 and L24 bombed a Boston trawler in the North Sea but failed to hit it. Then they flew over the Humber area. It was a warm, misty, foggy evening and they dropped bombs on Summercotes and Immingham but did little damage although one calf was killed at East Halton.

Army airships stopped coming over England at the end of 1916. Most of the Airships remaining in army service were taken over by the navy. They were mainly used for training purposes.

L13 came over Summercotes July 28th, 1916 at half past twelve and made for Nottingham. She flew over Fiskerton dropping bombs wherever a light showed but doing little damage except for broken windows. She passed directly out to sea over Boston two hours later. On another occasion, a Zeppelin followed a Hudson's bus to Fiskerton. When it stopped to unload, the airship dropped two bombs close by that landed on Longstones just outside Washingborough.

I was working on a farm at Ketton. That's about three miles out of Stamford. When a Zeppelin raid was imminent and before we could hear or see any sign of them, the pheasants would kick up a tremendous racket. We had a lot of guinea fowl too and they set up a racket as well as soon as the Zeppelins approached. The farmer thought he ought to kill them because he thought the crews in the airships would hear them and bomb the farm. When a bomb was dropped, it rattled all the windows and some cups fell off the table even though it had dropped four miles away.

Mrs Gwen Evans.

Extract from log of Zeppelin:

31.7.16. Came in and raided Lincs. Made for Newark dropping bombs along the route. No real damage caused.

On August 10th 1916, eleven airships raided the East coast from Kent to Yorkshire. L12 was hit by A/A (anti-aircraft) fire and came down in the sea. She was towed to Ostend by a German patrol boat but was attacked and destroyed by aircraft from Dunkirk. It was the twelfth Zeppelin lost up to that date.

L12 being towed into Ostend

There was no doubt that the Zeppelins frightened people. Few had even seen an aeroplane and there was mistrust about anything unnatural that flew.

I was coming back from the fields come mid-day when the sky grew dark and there weren't clouds in the sky that day. I turned round to see what was happening and there was this black shape coming straight towards me and it was making such a noise, a horrible roaring noise. I thought it was the devil himself and I didn't wait. I lifted my skirts and I ran. I ran down the steps to the vicar's cellar and I hid. I wasn't the only one either. There were quite a few of us and we were all scared near to death. Old Mother Johnson was that afeared, she had to loosen her stays. We didn't move until our men came home from work and fetched us."

Elsie Bellamy

We were out in the playground at school when we heard this noise. We looked up and saw this dark shape coming towards us. The girls ran indoors but we stayed and watched it coming nearer until the teacher came and rang the bell and made us all go into the class-room and shelter beneath our desks.

David Ellis

On September the 2nd, 1916 LZ90 was one of a 16 Zeppelin raid over Essex and Suffolk. She came in over Frinton at 11p.m. and wandered around flying over Wixloe at half past midnight. She was under attack from aircraft and escaped in cloud. They decided to lower the observation car and as it was lowering, the winch drive broke and the winch was rapidly picking up speed.

A crew member rammed an iron bar in the gears which caused a sudden stop. The cable could not stand the strain and snapped – not good for the unfortunate crew member. The winch was later discarded near Great Yarmouth and can now be seen at the Imperial War Museum. Either the cable broke or it was cut so that the car was released and the weight on the airship lessened as a result, which allowed it to gain height and get out of range of the attacking aircraft. It was hard luck for the observer in the cloud car.

Interesting Exhibit at Finsbury

In the course of one of the air raids over East Anglia a Zeppelin jettisoned, or lost, her observation car which was found, with some hundred of yards of the connecting wire, by a farmer next morning. A body was found inside.

He, like all the other observers were at the mercy of the wind and the weather. They were expected to tell the

Commander that a target was approaching and then they could be in the path of the bombs that were being released from the Zeppelin above them.

On September 12th 1916, LZ74 came in over the Essex coast and made for the dock area in London before flying over East Suffolk. It dropped its bombs indiscriminately including one on the Garratt works at Lieston. There was damage but no casualties.

Zeppelin L13 Naval Airship leaving Friedrichshafen for its North Sea Base, 1915

I was the elevator man on the L 13. Lieutenant Heinrich Mathy was our captain. It was a late September evening when we approached the British coast. The captain had held us out over the North Sea until the light began to fade. We went in by Wells next the Sea and crossed the Wash to Kings Lynn. It was a cold clear night and we could see the lights clear on the ground beneath us like beacons guiding us towards London. As we drew nearer to Cambridge, we could see the London lights on the horizon.

The captain ordered we increase our altitude to 2,500 meters, so I spun the elevator wheel bringing the nose to a slight upwards angle and carried on. It was cold. It was so cold that our sandwiches had frozen in our pockets and our eyebrows had turned white with the frost. We'd all got fur lined suits but they didn't keep out the cold at that height and we were all shivering but Mathy didn't seem to notice. He was staring through his binoculars all the time.

We didn't have anything to fear from the British planes. Their pilots weren't experienced night fighters and we had little to fear from the guns. They weren't likely to hit us at that height and if they did, they wouldn't have done much damage other than make a hole in the envelope or puncture the ballonet and we had a sail-maker who could repair that while we were flying. I wouldn't have wanted his job, having to scramble through the rigging and work at that height and in those conditions and he could only use one hand to support himself because he had to carry all the tools of his trade in the other, the rope with which to mend the tears, the needles and material.

We were all looking out at the scene beneath us. London was lit up. We were all shouting at the Captain telling him some good targets that we could see but he didn't take any notice. He was staring steadily through his binoculars. The centre of the city was partly blacked out but there was enough light for us to distinguish Regents Park and other places.

The captain ordered two bombs to be dropped. Then he dropped the big new, 300-kilogram explosive bomb and that caused a fire that lit up the town. Searchlights were weaving across the sky trying to find us but they didn't reach high enough and they didn't worry the captain. We bombed the warehouses by St Pauls. A shell came pretty near us so the Captain ordered me to go up to 3,500 metres. We started for home, leaving a huge fire behind us

Air ship L16's log:
2/3 September, 1916. Set out with 12 other airships to raid England. Over St Albans on way to bomb London saw SL11 go down in flames. Dropped bombs at Essenden and made for coast at 60 m.p.h.

L11 landing

September 2/3rd. 1916. The Zeppelins had had little to fear during these raids but British pilots had a new weapon; incendiary bullets. William Leefe Robinson was one of three pilots waiting to take off in his BE 2c aircraft at Sutton's Farm in Essex. He set off on the first patrol pursuing an airship that had been caught in searchlights. It took him nearly an hour to reach 10,000 feet which brought him close to the Zeppelin but he lost it when it flew into cloud. His endurance in the air was less than four hours. Robinson was about to abandon his patrol when he saw a red glow in the distance as bombs exploded. Leefe Robinson turned towards it although his fuel gauge was low.

Lt W L Robinson seated in his B.E.2c
The airmen are holding the original centre-section of the aeroplane's upper wing damaged by Robinson's own gun during the attack on the SL11

SL (Schutte Lanz type, another firm manufacturing airships) 11 was caught in the beams of searchlights and they held her despite her efforts to escape the light. The thunderous noise of the guns at Finsbury Park brought thousands of people out on to the streets to watch the spectacle above them, the huge, polished aircraft, the flashes of exploding shells, the drone of the engines and the crump of falling bombs produced a sight that many who saw it never forgot.

It seemed impossible to the watchers that the airship could escape the shell bursts but the Zeppelin was 11,500 feet up and the flak was not finding its target.

Caught in the searchlight

It was five minutes past two when Robinson saw the airship. He glanced at his petrol gauge and saw that he had barely fifteen minutes of flying time left. He had to move fast. Pushing his stick forward, he dived towards the airship. His single Lewis gun was mounted on a steel tube on the top wing in such a way that he could load and fire it from his piloting position. He clamped the stick between his knees and used both hands to clip the ammunition drum on to the gun. Metal sheathing prevented him from shooting his own propellers. He approached the airship head on and couldn't believe that there was no fire from it. He fired the length of the whole ship and was disappointed to see it flying steadily on. He used the second ammunition drum and tried again and again, there was no effect. Glancing at his fuel gauge, he realised he had only a few minutes flying time left. The Zeppelin had increased its speed and Robinson had to open his throttle to catch up with it. He decided on one last try. Fitting his last ammunition drum, he emptied it along the airship's beam, despairing of this new ammunition and the hopes that had been pinned on it. Then he saw the spot at which he had aimed begin to glow. Within seconds the airship was a burning inferno and falling to the ground. Robinson only just managed to get out of its path in time.

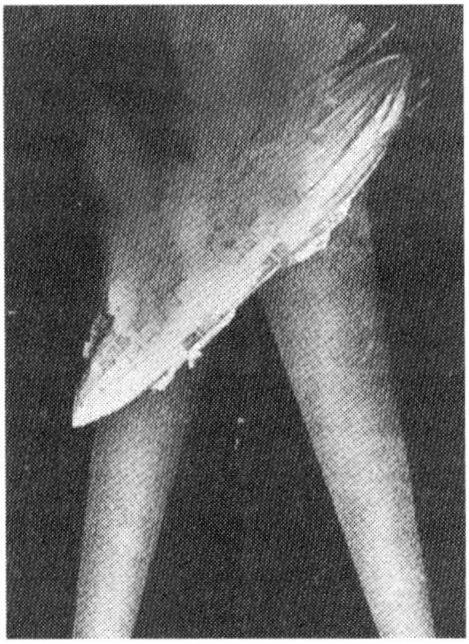

The SL11 going up in flames

One of the SL11's engines after the wreckage had burnt itself out

It came down near Cuffley on a hill which is now known as Zeppelin Hill, between St Andrew's Church, Castle Farm and the Plough Inn, the first one to be shot down by a British aeroplane over England. Thousands flocked to see what was left of it. Special trains ran from Kings Cross for the many people that wanted to visit the site. The inn keeper realised he was sitting at the entrance to an asset and charged two-pence entry fee to the site. Even Leefe Robinson had to pay.

An order was put out to arrest Leefe Robinson on a charge of murder. This was common practice for a pilot who had shot down an air ship. When men had died, the pilot was held responsible. There was such a public outcry that all charges against him were dropped. He was later awarded the Victoria Cross as a result of his actions that day.

The car is a prince Henry Vauxhall
Driving – Lt Leefe Robinson VC (shot down SL11 2/3 Sept 1916)
Front Passenger – Lt Sowry DSO (shot down L32 23/24 Sept 1916)
Rear LH side – Lt Tempest DSO (shot down L31 1/2 Oct 1916)

Dad came and woke us up and hurried us out into the street. We could hear the gun fire and Alice started to cry because she was frightened but, as soon as we got into the street, she stopped. We'd never seen anything like it. Everyone was out there and staring up at the sky and we weren't the only ones to still be in our night clothes. Old Mr Gottlieb was running up and down in his night shirt and a night cap on his head waving his fist at the big shadow in the sky and my friends thought he was a German spy but mother told me not to be so silly when I told her. It was the noise that frightened Alice. The gunfire deafened us and the flashes in the sky startled us. When there was a lull, we could hear the sound of the Zeppelin engines echoing above us. Then it disappeared behind a cloud and people went quiet for a bit. But the clouds cleared and we could see it again and the aeroplane that looked like a fly beside it. People were shouting and waving. It was like one big party. Then it caught light and it began to fall until it looked like a ball of fire. There was one huge cheer when it caught afire and then an uneasy silence fell over the crowd. Dad made us go back indoors then. He said that we'd seen history in the making. People went on celebrating. Old Mr Gottlieb was still there when Dad set off for work the next morning and he wasn't the only one.

On the 2nd of September 1916, L23 had set off from Nordholz. Its target was London but as it approached England, the weather deteriorated. There was heavy rain and hail and a strong wind was blowing so the Zeppelin altered direction and flew northwards up the coast, flying over Burnham Flats and over the Wash reaching the coast over Fosdyke at 10.40.p.m. turning over Gosberton and then on to Boston where it dropped its bomb load. Returning to base, the captain reported that he had bombed Norwich.

This brings so many memories back. My family were on the receiving end of the German bomb. My father was resident foreman and sluice keeper at the Grand Sluice drainage Depot and he was wounded in three places. My mother was cut about the face and my 18year old brother died from his injuries before reaching hospital. He had been hit in the stomach by shrapnel.

My father was a special constable and had been called out by the police. There was no public air raid warning at that time. He was talking to a friend, Mr George Beeton, at the Sluice Bridge when they heard the bomb falling and made for cover but they never made it. Mr Beeton was badly wounded and had his leg amputated that night. He was a railway shunter who lived in Argyle Street. Talking about it afterwards, we felt that the goods train departing over the crossing some time before the raid, directed the Zeppelin on to its target.

Mr Oughton.

September 23rd 1916.

Eleven Zeppelins set out to bomb England on the night of September 23rd, 1916. L17's target was Sheffield. In fact, it bombed Nottingham. It is thought that the German crew mistook the fires of shunting railway engines outside the Midland station for the glare of the blast furnaces in Sheffield. It wasn't the first time that Zeppelins had flown over the city but it was the first time it had been bombed.

The lookout saw the chimneys and fires at 12.40,a.m. and the Zeppelin immediately flew into a south west wind towards them. Mists in the Trent valley had hidden the airship. The first sighting was over Mapperley. It dropped one bomb there which fell in a garden in Robinson Road. Further bombs fell in Newthorpe Street, Lister Gate and a factory at Greyfriars Gate. Some incendiary bombs also fell on London Road station and Broadmarsh.

A young couple were asleep in their bed when an incendiary came through the roof and hit the husband, setting fire to the bed-clothes. They managed to get out of the house but the 21 year old man was in a state of collapse and was rushed to the hospital on a hand cart where he died. A 44 year old tailor's cutter and his wife were also killed. They had lived in Newthorpe Street. The couple had sons serving in France and were expecting them home on leave.

I was a miner at Gedling Colliery. We lived at Hyson Green and we heard the explosions. We wondered what was happening. My mother was terrified. As soon as we heard the Zeppelin flying on, I got dressed and went out. The Market Place and all down Wheeler Gate and Greyfriars Gate was crowded with people. It was like the Goose Fair. Everyone was saying that the Zeppelin had followed a train into the city. Everyone was blaming the railway for the raid.

The jury returned a verdict of murder by persons unknown and the coroner criticised the railway company for not extinguishing its lights.

The Zeppelin L33 came down in Essex at Little Wigborough. (see appendix 4 for wreck pictures) It had been hit by gunfire over England and the captain, realising that he would not make it to base had turned back because he preferred to land on the ground rather than on the sea. They landed near a cottage. It was in the middle of the night and the only sound that could be heard was the barking of the dogs at the cottage. The captain sent one of his crew to tell the occupants of the house that he was going to blow the Zeppelin up in ten minutes time but the people in the house refused to answer. So the captain ordered his crew to shoot the airship with Verey pistols, which they did but the Zeppelin did not ignite. So he then got them into marching order and they set off to march to Colchester, (the captain had worked there before the war).

L33 fuel tanks

That was when a warden, Edgar Nicholas, coming on duty met them. He heard the sound of marching boots first and got off his bike to see what was happening and met the column of Germans marching down the middle of the road and when he asked them where they thought they were going, the captain told him, “Colchester.” He ordered them to turn round and marched them down to the village hall. He was at a loss to know how to summon help. There were no telephones in the area and he couldn’t leave the Germans to go and fetch help himself. He heard a motor bike approaching and went out and stopped it, ordering the owner, Alfred Wright to go and fetch the army. The motor cyclist set off but it was still dark and he had to go over marshes which were liable to flooding. He hit a wall of water, came off his bike and was killed. It was another twenty four hours before help arrived at the village hall. Meanwhile, the warden had to bed the Germans down on the floor for the night.

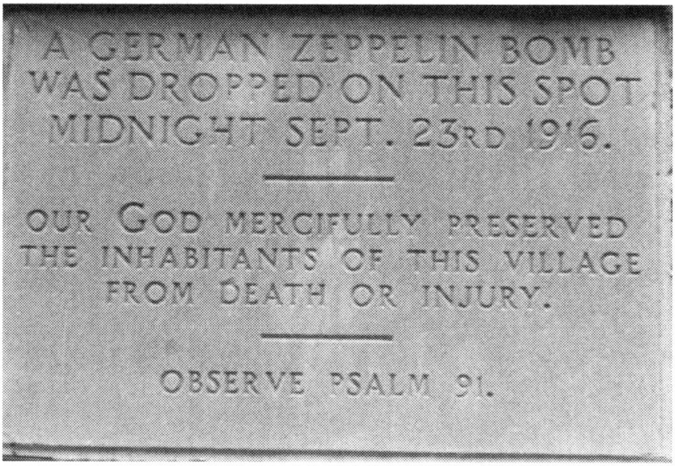

Memorial plaque - Facing post office opposite Dolands garage on Louth Road, Scartho. The Zeppelin concerned was the L13

The Zeppelins would cross the North Sea during the day, fix their positions visually and wait off the coast. At a time when navigation was planned through observation, it made it easier for them to make for their targets as dusk fell. The Admiral of the East Coast, Rear Admiral Ballard contacted Richard Bell Davies of the Royal Naval Air Service to see if the sea planes that were stationed at Killingholme could move nearer the coast so that they would be in a better position to attack the Zeppelins. As it was, the British planes did not have the range or the performance to attack the Zeppelins from a land base. Davies eyes fell on the Killingholme, one of the paddle steamers of the Humber ferry.

He decided that it would make an aircraft carrier if they adapted the top deck. It had a compass but it always pointed towards the funnel. The captain of a depot ship gave them a binnacle and the Killingholme was converted and set out for trials in the North Sea. The paddle steamers were not a success. Davies had already been sent out to France and was replaced by Arthur Longmore who did not share his enthusiasm for home made aircraft carriers.

But the Navy had not given up on the idea of launching a plane out to sea. They hit on the idea of towing a plane out into the North Sea and launching it from a lighter. It would then have enough range to attack the Zeppelin and the fire power to destroy it.

A flight deck of only 30 feet for Culle's Sopwith

A Canadian pilot, Lieutenant Stuart Culley was the man deputed for the job. The lighter on which his Sopwith Camel was tied down was towed out to sea at high speed by the destroyer,

H.M.S. Redoubt. It was a very uncomfortable journey. The sea was choppy and the lighter literally bounced over the waves.

The top of the lighter had been boarded over to make what must have been the smallest fixed wing flight deck in aviation history. It was thirty feet long and it had been calculated that if the destroyer towed the lighter at a speed of thirty knots, it would be enough for the Camel to take off.

The Harwich Naval Patrol Force operating from Harwich had set out on the evening of August 10th to act as a decoy to the Zeppelins. They sent out faked wireless messages to let the Germans know that they were there. Sure enough, the shadow of a Zeppelin was seen floating above the clouds and it was decided to launch the Camel.

The ground crew on the lighter faced almost as much danger as the pilot. There were no hand rails on the deck and the man who swung the propeller ran the risk of falling into the sea. The Bentley engine kicked into life and within minutes, the Sopwith Camel was heading towards the Zeppelin.

Although visibility on the sea was good, it was extremely bad in the air. There was a thick sea mist and the brilliant sunshine reflected on the haze which made the pilot's direction finding difficult. These conditions also affected the crew of the Zeppelin. The Commander was so occupied with watching the naval ships beneath him and, with the conditions affecting the sight of the crew, nobody on board noticed the tiny sea plane flying towards them. When they did see it, it was too late. L53 immediately changed course and started to climb but Culley forced his plane on.

He rose to 18,700 feet and attacked from beneath the airship. He sent seven rounds from his number one gun through the envelope but then the gun jammed and the Zeppelin was still flying. Then he sent his twin barrelled in from his number two gun, pushed forward his stick to escape from the big shadow above him. He was only just in time. L53 was engulfed in flames.

Three men were seen to jump from the Zeppelin, a distance of 18,000 feet, two of whom survived and were picked up. Cully then experienced the worst two hours of his life. The haze that had hidden him from the Zeppelin now hid the destroyer from him. He spent ages scouring the sea looking for it. He found it purely by chance and when he did land alongside it, there was only one pint of fuel left in the tank.

Culley, who was a Wing Commander in World War Two, was awarded the D.S.O. and the man who swung the propeller received the Air Force medal.

On October the 1st 1916, eleven Zeppelins set out to raid London but, because of the dreadful weather, fog, ice and sleet, none of them reached their target although Mathy who was the captain of L 31 came nearest. It was Mathy that was considered to be one of the best Zeppelin captains and who had inflicted so much damage on London in September but, this time, L31 did not return to base. It was shot down by a BE2c as it was forced lower by the ice forming on the envelope. His loss was keenly felt by the other Zeppelin crews but the problem went deeper. The Germans were facing a shortage of trained airship crews and many of those that were manning the airships were combat weary. In addition, they were facing greater dangers. The British were defending themselves more efficiently. There were more searchlights, better guns and aeroplanes that could match the heights at which the Zeppelins flew and they now had better trained and more experienced crews.

Zeppelin L31 being walked into the hangar

L31 1st/2nd October 1916

Heinrich Mathy

"Attack only with the protection of cloud cover or darkness," the Zeppelin commanders were told. The only other answer for them was to fly higher. The Zeppelins were stripped of everything that could possibly add to the weight of the airship. Things that made the crews' lives more comfortable such as wind shields were thrown out. The new ships did rise to terrific heights, up to 20,000 feet, well out of range of the British fighters. 'Height Climbers,' the British called them but the thermometers froze and the engines coughed and died. Much more important, was that the crews started to suffer from the effects of the cold and lack of oxygen and lost their efficiency. When the Zeppelins did reach England, they rarely found their targets.

Tyneside was an area of industrial importance with many munition works and factories working through the night and, as was often the case, glass panels were built into the roof. This meant they made an easy target and there were several raids by Zeppelins that were attracted by the lights. There was protection by searchlights, A/A guns and aircraft but communication and warning systems were poor. In some towns, the only telephone would be at the railway, generally at the signal box. There were several ways of telling local people that the airships were approaching. One village had a bugler, another used boy scouts to knock on doors and in others, knocker ups were employed to knock on people's windows.

Once a Zeppelin was heard, blind people would often be used to check the direction that the airship was travelling. Their hearing often proved to be more accurate than that of sighted people.

In November, 1916 Palmers Works at Jarrow suffered a serious attack. 18 men were killed and 72 injured by the shattered glass from the high factory roofs.

Ground crewmen reach up to catch the "grab-rails" as the airship comes to land.

On December 15th 1916, SS Apr was travelling from Hull to Yarmouth when they caught sight of a Zeppelin flying North, aiming towards Mablethorpe. The weather was rain and mist and the ships crew thought it was a bad day for the Zeppelin to be raiding England but no Zeppelin was recorded as coming overland that day.

Peter Strasser, Chief of the Naval Airship Division was still convinced of the Zeppelins importance and was sure that flying at the greater height would solve the problems that they were facing from the improved allied defences. The Zeppelin raids had reached their peak in 1916 and although they continued until the end of the war, there were fewer of them and their raids were less successful. In addition, their losses increased.

Anti aircraft gun crew at Trimley, Essex.
Zeppelins were attacked by aircraft and gun crews

In February, 1917, Army Zeppelin LZ 107 came in overland at Deal and circled near Dover and then Deal. The observation car was lowered 900 feet. Erich Zigan was the observer and the crew was unable to get him back on board because the winch had jammed so the unfortunate man had to ride back in the car over the North Sea, hoping that the Zeppelin would not lose gas and thus height because if it had he would have been in the records as the fastest boat on, or even under, the sea. It took seven hours to get back to base and a rough landing and he was hanging 900 feet below. These men were probably the first kama-kazi pilots. The Zeppelin lowered the cloud car. The ground crew cut the cable. The officer was released, then the Zeppelin landed.

By 1917, Zeppelin raids over England had become less frequent. This was because so many of the airships had been damaged or destroyed and because of the improved performances of allied aeroplanes.

There was a five Zeppelin raid on the night of March 16th, 1917. L35 commanded by Ehrlich came in over Broadstairs and released 20 bombs, three of which weighed 660 pounds but they fell in open fields and little damage was done. On the return flight, she flew into a heavy snowstorm which caused an engine to fail and the heavy weight of the snow brought the Zeppelin down low. She made a heavy landing at Dresden and damaged her framework which took three months to repair.

L39 was commanded by Koch and came in over Margate and flew back out to sea over Pevensey Bay having released six bombs which had damaged two cottages. Navigation was poor and she was next seen over the French battlefields. The Commander immediately ordered all engines to be stopped to avoid detection. She was cruising at 10,000 feet and going along with the wind but she had already been seen by the French AA and they opened fire on her. The crew battled to restart the engines so that they could escape but they refused to start because of the frost. Over a hundred shells were fired at her and she came down at Campagne at 5.30 a.m. All of the 17 crew perished.

L 41 came in over Winchelsea, dropping bombs near Rye and Camber, reporting back that they had bombed Harwich. They flew into a heavy snowstorm on the way back which made the airship very heavy with snow and ice. They managed to reach base and land with a lot of difficulty.

On the 14th of May 1917 a H12 flying boat, number 1866, set off from Great Yarmouth on a routine patrol. Flt. Sub Lt. Leckie was the pilot, Flt. Sgt Galpin was the navigator, Chief Petty Officer was the wireless operator and observer and Air Mechanic O.R.Laycock was the engineer. The flying boat was armed with three Lewis guns and carried four 100lb bombs.

Curtis H.12 flying boat

Setting off at 3.30.a.m. they went in the direction of the Terschilling light-ship. They stopped using the wireless when they were eighty miles out to avoid being traced by the enemy. Thirty minutes later, they saw a Zeppelin dead ahead of them. They were flying at 6,000 feet and they reckoned that the Zeppelin was flying at 3,000 feet. The flying boat crew prepared to attack. They jettisoned three of the bombs they were carrying to lessen their weight and to give them more manoeuvrability and speed of climb. They increased their speed to 75 knots. Petty Officer Whatling took up position to man the rear gun and Flt. Sgt-Lt Galpin manned the two forward Lewis guns.

The Zeppelin, L22 started to climb when the flying boat was within half a mile of it. Until then, the airship crew had been unaware of the impending attack. The aircraft dived at 90 knots, approaching slightly astern before levelling out and flying alongside, slightly below the control car. They raked the envelope with incendiary bullets from a 50 yard range before their two forward guns jammed. The aircraft flew off to free their guns and prepare for another attack when they saw a glow in the airship envelope. Its tail was hanging down at an angle of forty-five degrees and within five seconds, the ship was alight and falling tail first. Two men were seen to jump from the tail gun position and a third from the gondola. None of them had parachutes. The whole Zeppelin was burnt to a skeleton within fifty seconds from the first glow. It plunged into the sea and the only sign that it had existed was a black patch on the surface and a column of brown smoke.

The aircraft returned to base with a few bullet holes in the wing and on the rear fuselage. This was the first time that a Zeppelin had been destroyed by a flying boat.

23 May 1917

L44 drifted over Harwich at approximately 18,000 feet. Temperature was 40 degrees centigrade below zero. The engines had stopped and the crew were helpless with sickness because of the high altitude. It drifted out a long way across the North Sea where the crew began to come round. They managed to start two of the engines and made for their base.

There was a seven Zeppelin raid on the night of 16th June 1917 when L48 was shot down on its maiden flight by 2nd Lieutenant Watkins in a BE 12. It crashed at Holly Tree Farm, Theberton, Suffolk. Three of the crew survived including L.T.Meith who was the second in command. Both his legs were broken. The three survivors were nearly trampled on by the terrified horses in the field. Fourteen of the crew perished.

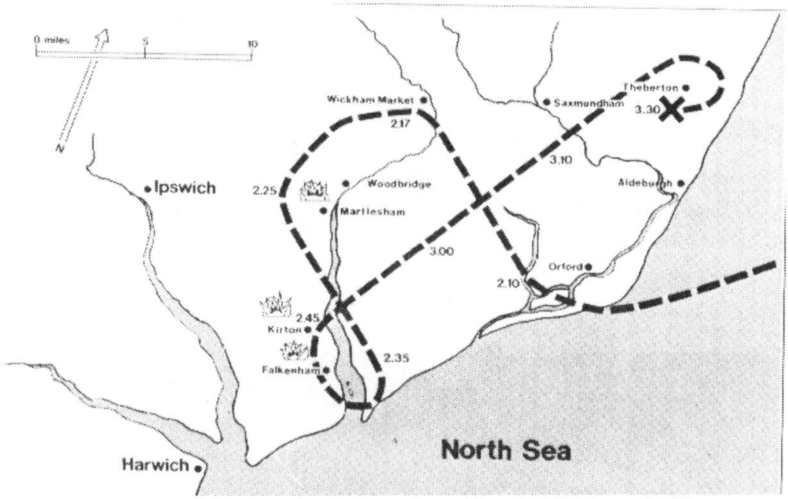

The route taken by the L48 on the night of 16/17 June 1917

Skeleton of an airship

Theberton Church near to L48 Zepp crash site

The Coroner and Jury of the Theberton inquiry

An open-air inquest

The inquest was held because of the 'murders' of the air crew that had been committed by Watkins.

The L48 on a Suffolk field. Note the cordon of military guards around the wreckage and the spectators on the path

Mr G Greenacre who lived at Theberton in 1917 & visited the zepp L48 crash site on the night

Mr Greenacre was in bed and, heard what sounded like hundreds of empty tin cans falling. He looked out and saw flames. He put his trousers and jacket over his pyjamas and got on his bike to cycle towards the flames but he was not on his own. Hundreds were on their way there and soon the army arrived

L48 Theberton, loading up the nose

Left, the tail

The crew members that died were buried at Theberton but later on, like other of their comrades that died on British soil, were removed and laid to rest in Cannock Chase.

German cemetery at Cannock Chase, Staffs

Two Zeppelins, L 42 and L46 approached at a very high altitude on 23rd of June. The Commander of the Airship Service, Peter Strasser was on board the L 42. They circled the area but dropped no bombs and returned to base. Both crews were ill through lack of oxygen and had difficulty moving about. One of the crew died on the return journey. Strasser realised the problems of high altitude flying and that the oxygen breathing apparatus that was supplied was useless. Engine trouble developed and the mechanics were too cold and too numb to attempt to repair them.

On 21/22 August 1917 there was an eight Zeppelin raid. They bombed Hull at 20,000 feet and only one man was injured. The only bombs recorded on the raid were around Hull.

On the night of 19th of October 1917, the last raid of the year took place, the SILENT RAID.

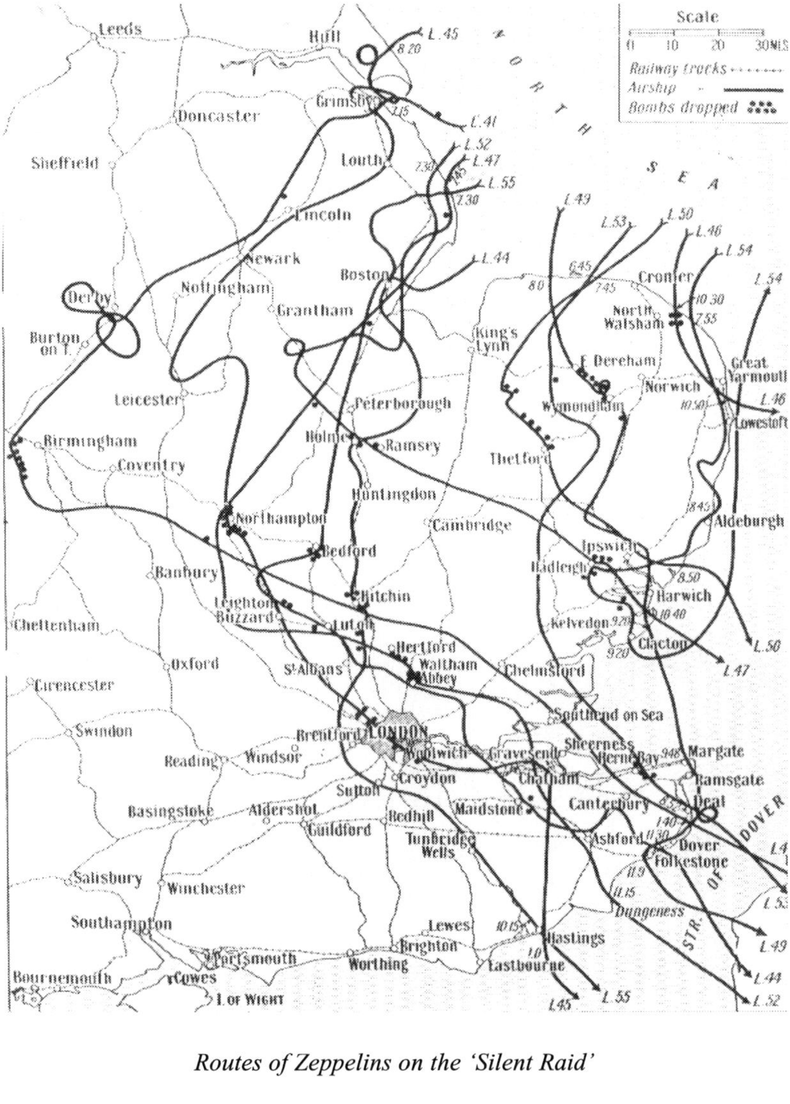

Routes of Zeppelins on the 'Silent Raid'

Strong winds had been blowing at the German base making lift off difficult. A depression was approaching from Iceland and a raging gale was blowing from NNW at 20,000 feet while still air lower down held a layer of mist and fog. It was calm at ground level. It was very quiet and people on the ground did not hear the Zeppelins flying overhead. That was why it was known as the Silent Raid.

L41, L 44, L45, L 46, L 47, L49, L50, L52, L53, L54, L55 set off to bomb the central industrial areas of Britain - Sheffield, Manchester, Liverpool and Hull. L42 and L51 should have been on the raid but they could not leave their sheds due to the strong cross winds.

L41 dropped high explosive bombs at Waltham, Caistor, North Carlton and Scampton before flying on to Derby but she could not find her target so dropped bombs to the west of Birmingham which fell between Netherton and Burnt Green.

L 50, note the black painted underside designed to conceal the ship from English searchlights

Three fell on the Austin works at Longbridge. Bombs were dropped near Lincoln, killing two sheep. She flew home over the Franco/ Belgian battlefields, circling overhead as if lost before she flew on to Germany. L 44 was shot down by the French anti aircraft guns at Chenneviers. There were no survivors. L 45 was forced down at Sisterton. The crew set fire to their Zeppelin. 17 crew were taken prisoner. L50 made an emergency landing at Montigny-le-Roy and the craft broke up on landing. Part of it, with four men still on board broke away and took off in the wind and was lost over the sea. The remaining crew of 16 men were taken prisoner.

L49 was shot down by French flying corps at Bourbonne-les-Bains. 19 crew were taken prisoner.

The first raid of 1918 was on the 12th of March when five Zeppelins flew over the East Riding and Hull area. L53 bombed Hull where one woman died of a heart attack during the raid, then bombed Grimsby and Howden. 10 aircraft were sent up to intercept it but were unable to reach the airship's altitude. Two planes crashed on landing Two members of the crew died from carbon monoxide poisoning on the return journey. L 54 set out to bomb the Midlands with L61, L62 and L 63. She reached the Yorkshire coast before ten p.m. but did not come overland, dropping her bombs in the sea before returning to base. She reported that she had bombed Hull.

On March 13th, L42 raided West Hartlepool. Factory lights were shining, as were those in the streets and houses. 15 bombs were dropped. 8 people were killed and 39 injured before the airship was chased out to sea by FE2D aircraft. They were unable to reach the Zeppelin's altitude.

On April 7th 1918, L59 was struck by lightning and came down in the sea.

The raid on April 12/13th was the last one to drop bombs by Zeppelins on British soil. It was a five Zeppelin raid, all of them the most modern L 60s models; L60, L61, L62, L63, L64.

Peter Strasser was on board L 60. It came in over Spurn Point and dropped bombs on East Halton and Thornton Saxby, flying at 16,000 feet. Most of the bombs dropped on open ground. The Commander reported bombing Leeds. She never undertook another raid. On 19th of July, she was bombed in her shed at Tondern by an aircraft that had taken off from H.M.S. Furious, a ship that had been converted to an aircraft carrier. Captain Smart carried out the raid in a Sopwith Camel and landed successfully back on board.

Herbert Ehrlich was the Commander of L61. He flew directly to Sheffield at 16,400 feet but he never noticed the city because it was blacked out and there was heavy cloud so the Zeppelin flew to the south of it, heading straight for Liverpool. Turning north at Runcorn, she released all her bombs on a town that was well lit up by blast furnaces - Wigan. Railway property and houses were destroyed. 8 people were killed and 13 injured.

Hauptmann Manger was Commander of L62. He reported coming in over Mablethorpe but he actually flew over Norfolk. He claimed that he had bombed a night flying aerodrome near Lincoln. It was Tydd St Mary. He then made for Coventry and Birmingham where he dropped two and a half tons of bombs although there was little damage. An FE2b of 38 squadron, piloted by Lt. Noble Campbell chased the airship and came within firing range and shot at the Zepp which returned the fire, hitting the pilot in the head. He managed to make a forced landing near Coventry and survived. It was the only time that a Zeppelin crew had wounded an attacking pilot. There were strong headwinds and the Zeppelin had to come down to 11,000 feet, She was attacked by A/A fire near Norwich and, despite being damaged and running short of gas, managed to limp back to base.

L63 with Captain von Freudenreich in command, came over the Wash near Skegness. Her first bombs were dropped to the east of Metheringham. Four bombs were dropped at Waddington Mere and four on a farm at Navenby (Mr Priestley's), hitting a stable and killing two horses. Bombs were also dropped at Blankney. She flew towards Lincoln but was fired on by Brauncewell A/A guns so she turned away dropping more bombs at Fleet and Little Sutton. Despite developing engine trouble, she managed to limp home and survived the war only to be destroyed by her own crew so that she would not come into the possession of the victorious countries.

L 64, commanded by Kapitan Schutze, came in over the Wash and made straight for Lincoln but Lincoln had received a warning so the city was blacked out. Lights were still showing in Doddington and Skellingthorpe. Bombs were dropped on both these villages causing many broken windows and damage to property but no injuries. More bombs were dropped in the Waddington area most of which fell on farm land. The Zeppelin was having serious engine problems due to gas loss. Ballast had to be released. Reaching base, the ship made a heavy landing, causing damage and was out of action for many weeks. In July 1920, she was flown to England by her crew, landing at Pulham Airship base. She never flew again.

Only one more raid was ever attempted on August 5th 1918.

L53,L56, L65 and the brand new L70 approached our coast at 16,500 feet. The L70 class was the most technically advanced airship of World War One It could fly higher and faster and was capable of carrying a 10 ton bomb load over long distances. It was claimed that it could fly to New York, bomb the city and return to base without landing or refuelling.

The airships were spotted by the crew of the Leman Tail lightship. Captain Robert Leckie and Major Edgar Cadbury (of chocolate bar fame) were scrambled to attack from Yarmouth Air-base at 10p.m.

Major Cadbury was attending a concert with his wife when he saw his orderly in the aisle.

"Do you want me?" he asked.

"Yes Sir. There are three Zeppelins overheard."

Cadbury dashed by car to the air station. One of the DH4s had already taken off and he climbed into the second machine, snatching his flying jacket, scarf, goggles and helmet from his batman. Robert Leckie, the commander of the flying boat squadron had not expected to fly that night. He had no flying kit, not even gloves. He didn't hesitate and hopped into the gunman's seat beside Cadbury and they were away.

Major Edgar Cadbury

As soon as they were airborn, Cadbury jettisoned his bombs to rid himself of the weight. Their DH4 approached L70 head on. Major Cadbury flew alongside the gondola, Captain Leckie fired his Lewis gun and, almost immediately, the Zeppelin became a ball of flame, falling into the sea on the approach to the Wash, 8 miles north of Wells next the Sea. Peter Strasser, the head of the Naval Airship Division had been on board and perished with the crew. He had been responsible for the building of these advanced Zeppelins, convinced that they would help Germany win the war but, by then, the airship as a war machine had seen its day.

Edgar Cadburys DH4

Cadbury and Leckie then went on to attack L65 but their gun jammed and the airship escaped back to base after releasing her bombs into the sea which allowed her to climb to 19,400 feet. Nine aircraft were up that night from Great Yarmouth and Burgh Castle. It is thought that the L65 had been damaged by Jardine and Munday flying a DH9. Unfortunately they both perished when they landed on the burning sea. It is understood that they thought they were landing on a flight path.

The service faced disaster on 5th January, 1918 when five Zeppelins and four new hangars were destroyed in a fire – The Ahlhorn Disaster, 15 were killed and 134 injured.

Victims of air raids were given military funerals, - a firing party with a salvo over the grave and a bugler playing the last post. The coffin was draped with a Union Jack and was accompanied by a band playing the Dead March.

1,414 people were killed and 3,416 injured by air raids in the First World War. In the year preceding the outbreak of the war, 2,099 people were killed and 42,544 injured in traffic accidents while 1,000 were killed and 150,000 injured in the mining industry.

8,500 bombs were dropped on England from lightweight incendiaries to the high explosives that weighed up to a ton.

Appendix 1 - Zeppelin crews

Zeppelin crews were all officers or NCOs. All of them were volunteers, sailors who had proved their their ability to withstand sickness, cold and wet conditions, common sense thinking and acting responsibility, comradeship; they were volunteers not conscripted.

They trained for six months, as a crew consistently checked on agreeability and team work, in the air. They were checked on flying in rarified air and bitter cold conditions and oxygen use, or lack of. Once they passed the course they remained as a crew from Zepp to Zepp, only Commanders changed.

They all became officers or NCO's.

The mechanics probably kept the warmest but had to suffer with the excessive noise and fumes of fuel and oil from the engine.

The crew were allowed 50 grammes of rum or brandy (for above 3000 metres). Their rations would be cold potato, bread, sausage, hard-boiled eggs, chocolate bars, biscuits and crackers. They also had self-heating tinned food of soup or stew. The mechanics fitted hot plates on the exhaust manifolds for heating food, boiling water and frying eggs or to defrost their frozen sandwiches.

A crew consisted of 16 to 23 according to ship size:

Crew member	Responsibilities
The Commander	Airship, targets, bomb release and selection i.e. incendiaries or He
Executive Officer (in rear gondola)	Walking ship in and out of hangar. Conveying orders from Commander to Crew. Allocation of watch duties etc.
Chief Engineer	In charge of mechanics, steersman. Machine guns, Sailmaker and smooth operation of the ship.
Observation Officer	In charge of wireless / telegraph. Operation of bombing equipment etc
Wireless operators	Sending and receiving of orders, plus messages and navigation advice (plus machine gun operation)
Steersman: 1 operator of rudders, 1 operator of elevators	Also operated hydrogen valves and ballast release. Also machine gun operators.
Sailmaker	for all gas cells and outer cover, gas automatic release valves and manual valves.
Observation car operator	Possibly a radio operator
Mechanics	For an engine – smooth operation, throttle settings, clutching prop in/out, oiling exposed working components. In flight they had to do repairs (major and minor), pumping fuel and oil to gravity tanks inside the airship, also coolant to radiators and radiator grille flap adjusting.

Appendix 2

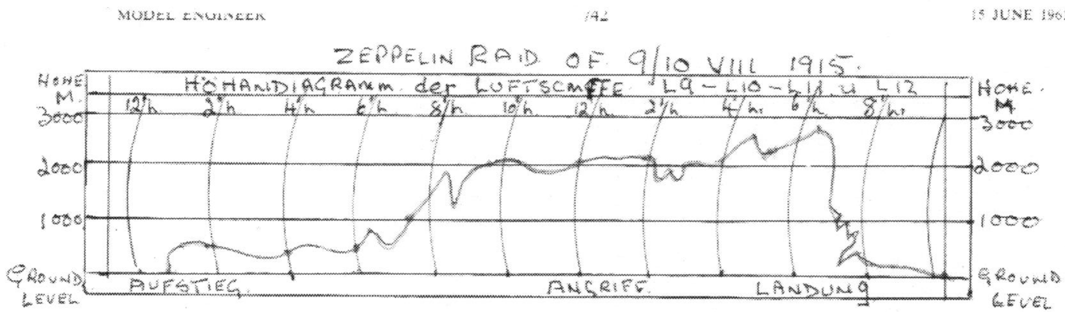

This chart was a record of the L10 Zeppelin flight for 9/10th August 1915.
The flight was accurately timed by watch.
The heights were recorded by an altimeter and barograph.
Ground level varies according to base location

L10 takes the air at about 12.45pm. The hydrogen warms and expands but cools at 500 meters over the North Sea which is a safe area from attack, but five hours over the sea, danger could exist. Some fuel is used up, so it is possible to gain a safer height. Between 8pm and 4am the Zeppelin was over England. The dips could be caused by flying through damp clouds. After 4am, the sun would warm the hydrogen giving more lift. The dip here could again be flying through damp cloud but in the sun again around 6am and in a safe area. At nearly 3000 meters, the automatic gas valves may have opened releasing gas to prevent the gas cells bursting. As the Zeppelin has dropped its bombs and is now low on fuel it would gain height and its better to release gas well before landing so it clears with less risk of explosions from static electric sparks of engine sparks from idling engines. Landed at around 9am.

Total time airborne, around 20 hours and would have covered around 900 miles at 45mph

Appendix 3

Builder no	Service no	Date destroyed	Remarks
SL11	SLAA	3.9.16	Shot down in flames by a BE2c. Crashed on 'Plough Hill', Cuffley, Herts. All 16 crew members killed
LZ25	ZIX	8.10.14	Bombed in Dusseldorf shed by a Sopwith Tabloid 168
LZ37	LZ37	7.6.15	Bombed in mid-air by a Morane Saulnier Crashed on convent at Ghent, Belgium. Nine killed
LZ38	LZ38	7.6.15	Bombed in Brussels-Evere shed two Henry Farmans
LZ61	L21	28.11.16	Shot down in flames by a BE2c. Disappeared into sea 10 miles E of Lowestoft. All 17 crew members killed
L64	L22	14.5.17	Shot down in flames by a Curtiss H12 flying boat. Disappeared at sea 18 miles NNW of Texel Island. All 21 crew members killed.
LZ66	L23	21.8.17	Shot down in flames by a Sopwith Pup. Disappeared into the sea. All 21 crew members killed
LZ72	L31	2.10.16	Shot down in flames by a BE2c. Crashed on Oakmere Farm, Potters Bar, Herts. All 19 crew members killed
LZ74	L32	24.9.16	Shot down in flames by a BE2c. Crashed on Snail's Hall Farm, near Great Burstead, Essex. All crew members killed

Builder's no	Service no	Date destroyed	Remarks
	L33	23.9.16	Shot down by gun fire and landed in in Essex at Little Wigborough
LZ78	L34	28.11.16	Shot down in flames by a BE2c at 10,000ft. Disappeared beneath the sea. All 20 crew members killed.
LZ92	L43	14.6.17	Shot down in flames by aCurtis H12 flying boat. Disappeared into sea off Vlieland. All 24 crew members killed
LZ95	L48	17.6.17	Shot down in flames by a BE12. Crashed on Holly Tree Farm, near Theberton, Suffolk. 14 crew members killed, 3 survivors
LZ99	L54	19.7.18	Bombed in Toska shed, Tondern by 3 Sopwith 2F1 Camels.
LZ100	L53	11.8.18	Shot down in flames by a Sopwith 2F1 Camel. Disappeared into sea. 19 crew members killed, 1 man leapt from 19,000 feet and survived. He was picked up by a Dutch vessel
LZ108	L60	19.7.18	Bombed in Toska shed by 3 Sopwith 2F1 Camels
LZ112	L70	5.8.18	Shot down in flames by a DH4 A8032. Disappeared into sea off Cromer. All 22 crew members killed

Appendix 4 - Airship raids, Autumn 1916

Map drawn to show the course taken by raiding Zepps over the east and south-east of England in August and September 1916

Appendix 5 – The following four pictures are all of the wreck of the L33 , Little Wigborough, Essex

Appendix 6 –wreck pictures of L32, 24 September 1916
Billericay, Essex